Small Time

A Life in the Football Wilderness

Justin Bryant

**BENNION
KEARNY**

Published by Bennion Kearny Limited
6 Victory House, 64 Trafalgar Road
Birmingham, B13 8BU

www.BennionKearny.com

Cover image: ©Justin Bryant

Justin Bryant was born in Melbourne, Florida, in 1966. He graduated from Elon University with a Bachelor's degree in English and from New York University with a Master of Fine Arts Degree in Creative Writing. He is the author of the novel 'Season Of Ash' (ENC Press, 2004). His short fiction has appeared in numerous journals, and he has written about football for XI Quarterly and The Howler. As a goalkeeper, he played for clubs on both sides of the Atlantic. He is a qualified goalkeeper coach and is currently Director of Goalkeeping at NC State University. He lives in Raleigh, North Carolina, with his dog Blake, an American pit bull terrier.

Introduction

The sun is not yet high but it's already hot, burning the dew off cobwebs in wild grasses lining tidal canals. A flock of roseate spoonbills stands in a shallow pond which reflects thunderheads already building on the horizon. From a deeper pond on the other side of the footpath comes a splash. I turn and see what I've been looking for: a huge alligator slides from the bank into black water and cruises away toward the mangroves. I raise my camera and aim the heavy telephoto lens. The gator sinks beneath the surface.

I'm in the Merritt Island National Wildlife Refuge on the east coast of Florida. 140,000 acres of wetlands and trails, it harbors eagles, ospreys, wild boars, manatees, and bobcats. It is popular with serious birders, but I come to see the gators. I'm fascinated by their sheer improbability, these Jurassic river dragons gliding through ponds and canals encircling the rockets of the Kennedy Space Center. They are apex predators, and I envy the alpha status they enjoy in their sun-soaked, oceanside paradise.

Though I'm normally a late sleeper, I'm happy to rise before the sun to come here. It's my only chance to relax, to be alone; it's the only time that the knots that twist deep in my gut seem to unbind.

The gator surfaces, facing me, thirty yards away. I take a series of pictures before he loses interest and swims off. The heat rises. It's July, which means sun and heat, bristling thunderstorms, swords of blue-white lightning. A whimper of breeze, stifled by humidity, comes from the ocean, and sweat drips from my hair.

Introduction

I look at my watch: 9:47 am. I remember the game – we play at 7:30 pm – and my stomach tightens with the first familiar twitch of nerves.

I have come to recognize that there is an obvious metaphor at play here. The Merritt Island National Wildlife Refuge is every bit a refuge for me as much as it is for the animals. For a start, it's a refuge from illness. In 1989, while battling for a contract with the Orlando Lions of the American Soccer League, my nervous system collapsed, taking much of my digestive system function with it. I nibble and graze like a prairie mammal, unable to eat a full meal in one sitting. Still unwell, I resumed my career in the cold and damp of Scotland and England for a few years. I came home in 1994 looking as sick as I felt, my skin the color of uncooked pasta, my eyes ringed in permanent shadow. But it didn't take long for the Florida sun to bring some life back into my complexion, and I soon began to chase it, as if the sun could cook away whatever toxins were plaguing me.

The refuge gives me a break from people, too. I like people. I have close friends, and I live with my girlfriend on a tropical plot of land between two rivers on South Merritt Island. But I have overpowering urges to be alone. I can't predict when the urge will strike, but if it does so at a time I can't accommodate it, I have to fight off a panic attack. Sociability is one of the greatest stressors of playing a team sport, especially as a job, where I have to train and play and travel with twenty other people at close quarters, and it goes a long way toward explaining why I'm a goalkeeper. We tend to get left alone.

Primarily, the wildlife refuge is a respite from football, a game I still love but which has become the source of a deep and churning conflict. The team framework - the schedule, the rules, the travel - is stifling.

The physical demands, especially in the Florida summer, and with my health still far from optimum, are punishing. On the other hand, we play in front of crowds, small but enthusiastic, and crowds feed the one part of me that remains healthy: my ego. Kids ask for my autograph after games. Some of them wait until later, standing by my car, waiting for me to walk up in street clothes. It's embarrassing; I'm not even a fulltime pro, just a goalkeeper for the Cocoa Expos, playing for $50 a game in another crapshoot pre-MLS American league. But I don't tell them that; they're just kids, so I act the part. I sign and pose for pictures and then drive away, ego glowing.

I check the time again: 10:30. I have all day, but I know I can't stay out here for long in the heat and withering sun if I want to have enough energy to play well. I fantasize about staying in the wildlife refuge. I've brought food to nibble at, and my truck, an old Toyota 4Runner, has an enclosed bed that I can sleep in. It's 1995 and people have cell phones now, but I do not. Nobody can reach me out here.

Thunderheads continue to swell on the horizon, gray and bruised with moisture, primed with electricity. Maybe they'll grow. Maybe the match will be cancelled. But I've already checked the forecast. The storms will be long gone before sunset.

I can't keep the match out of my mind. I might not love playing these days, but I'm still competitive and still invest a big part of my self-worth into how I play, what fans and opponents and my teammates think of me as a player. Every time I think about the match, my stomach contracts. So many unknowns when you play in goal, so much beyond your control. So many potential disasters.

Introduction

An osprey cries from a dead tree. I raise my camera. It's looking right at me, eyes black and glossy, head tilted.

No use. I'm too distracted by the game, checking my watch every five minutes. I pack my camera, drive home, and pass the rest of the day napping fitfully. I force myself to choke down half a meal. I don't eat well on match days. Or most days.

The match itself, when it finally comes, passes in a blur. I play mostly on instinct now, do almost everything right without conscious thought. At twenty-eight, I'm five or more years older than most opposition players. They're fresh out of university, sure that this is the first step toward professional stardom, and almost certainly wrong. It's not going to happen for most of them, but I don't need to be the one to tell them. The world in general, and professional football in particular, has worked out a very efficient system of dishing out reality checks. I've been hardened by this knowledge in a way they haven't yet, and with it comes an exoskeleton of confidence, borne of knowing I have survived the worst the game could throw at me. It's ironic, but now that I no longer *need* to play the game, no longer live to play it, I'm playing better than I ever have before.

There are still moments of crystalline joy in every game, reminders of why I continue to play, when so much of what surrounds the game feels like a chore. Something as simple as a well-struck goal kick sends endorphins flooding through my body, and the feeling of cleanly catching a hard shot – the ball sticking in my gloves with an audible *squeak* – is positively euphoric. Sometimes during a match, I'll look down at my gloves and think, "Somebody made these specifically to make my life easier." For a goalkeeper, there is nothing like the smell of a new pair of gloves. And you never forget your first pair.

We win, as always, although it was close this time. We have just won the Eastern Division championship. I don't know who we beat. All these teams have long since blurred together. After the final whistle, I sign my autographs and mingle with the fans and a few friends, but I don't linger. I remember that this isn't just another game; there is a showdown looming, and I've got a front-row seat.

The dressing room is noticeably silent as we shower and change into street clothes, the usual post-game chatter and jokes replaced by a sort of nervous hum as players speak in whispers. Finally, Dave Mackey, a defender I've played with for years, stands in the center of the room, addresses the team's management – Cocoa Expo owner Rick Sandt and his assistant, Colin Thomas – and asks the question we've all been wondering for weeks: why haven't we been paid?

I knew this was coming, was secretly thrilled, but it's also terribly awkward, because I have a secret: I *have* been paid. The team's other goalkeeper quit halfway through the season, and I leveraged my position of strength and threatened to walk away, leaving them with nobody to play in goal, unless they paid all past-due money: $650. Colin had no choice but to write me a check. So when Dave Mackey starts walking around the room, pointing at each one of us and saying, "…and *he* hasn't been paid, and *he* hasn't been paid, and *he* hasn't been paid," I meet his eye but feel like a scab who's crossed union picket lines. I've been paid, Dave. Sorry.

I don't have long to worry about that, though. After listening patiently for a few minutes, Sandt suddenly leaps to his feet and bellows, "Stop right there! You're not going to blackmail me! Anybody who thinks they're going to blackmail me, there's the door!" He points vaguely in the direction where a door might be. He's not a young man, wears bottle-thick glasses and ill-fitting shorts. He has always reminded me of Nixon, post-Watergate, walking the beaches of San Clemente with a dog more interested in chasing seagulls than being his pal. He's getting more furious by the moment, doing a strange sort of hop from foot to foot as he sputters and fumes about being blackmailed. Dave is so stunned by this performance that for a moment he is silent, almost smiling, before calmly insisting that nobody is being blackmailed. We just want our money.

Standing in the background, watching on with a look of dignified horror, is Ricky Hill. Over four hundred appearances for Luton Town as a midfielder, three full England caps, winner of the League Cup in 1988, Ricky played in an era when black players occasionally had bananas thrown at them. He handled such moments with somber grace. After retiring as a player, he went into coaching, but found opportunities in Britain limited, to say the least. Every one of the ninety-two professional teams in England was managed by a white man. So he came to the States to get experience. We're lucky to have him. All the players love him. But it seems as if it's now, at the tail end of the season, in the middle of this bizarre performance from Sandt, that he realizes what he's gotten himself into.

There is an added complication to the hostilities: despite the unilateral nonpayment, a handful of players are still loyal to Sandt, and they begin undermining Dave with objections and qualifications. This is rooted in a few related things: they all played for Sandt at university, when he ran the program at Florida Tech, and they're all British. We get along fine, the Yanks and Brits, but the Brits tend to close ranks when things go wrong. Once they do this, the confrontation with Sandt fizzles to a pathetic end. I make eye contact with Keith Ames, my closest friend on the team.

It is an accusatory look. It is Keith who, the previous spring, talked me into playing for the Expos. He grins sheepishly.

When I get home, there is a message on my answering machine from a reporter at *Florida Today*, the local newspaper. He wants my thoughts on the upcoming playoffs. The thought of more games to come makes my stomach hurt. My stomach that lurches and groans day after day, and no doctor can tell me why it's broken.

I erase the message, take a deep breath, and phone Ricky Hill to tell him I'm quitting.

1

I was born in Melbourne, Florida in 1966. Pele came to the New York Cosmos in 1975, so for the first decade of my life, 'football' meant only the American variety: gridiron. I had seen European football on TV, on a program called "Soccer Made in Germany" which aired at irregular times. I had no interest in playing the game, but I was fascinated by the accuracy of the passing. I had always assumed footballers merely kicked the ball as hard as possible and hoped it went in the right direction (I will later play in leagues where this is indeed the case), and was impressed by how often the ball appeared to go exactly where the player who kicked it had intended. It made an impression, but no more than that.

It wasn't until I took notice of the burgeoning North American Soccer League that my mild interest morphed into infatuation. The first American soccer revolution was underway. Pele transformed the New York Cosmos into a global brand, and down in Florida, we had the Tampa Bay Rowdies drawing 40,000 fans to Tampa Stadium. Suddenly, soccer wasn't just happening somewhere far away, in drab, cold Europe, but in the sunshine and kaleidoscopic color of 1970s America. Rowdies games were broadcast live on Channel 44. I watched each one, screaming at the TV, living and dying with every result. I covered my walls with pictures of every player on the team. I began playing the game with other kids in the neighborhood, and I – all of us – became obsessed.

Luckily, my mother encouraged this interest. With her blessing, I built a small pitch on one side of our backyard, and a full-sized goal on the other side. We churned away every blade of grass and nicknamed the pitch 'The Dust Bowl'. I found I was a natural, could soon shoot with both feet, dribble at pace, do tricks and juggle a ball endlessly. I wasn't exactly inclined to modesty, and couldn't ignore the fact that I soon dominated my friends. But I was strangely attracted to playing in goal, and found that I loved flinging myself after shots, even in the hot dirt of the Dust Bowl.

I joined my first official youth team at twelve, playing both in goal and outfield positions, but after a few games, my mind was made up: I didn't trust anyone else in goal, and wanted the job for myself. My team was loaded with all the best players in our age group, as sometimes happens with youth teams, and I played four or five games before conceding my first goal, from a penalty. When it beat me, I howled with real despair. It was the worst feeling I'd ever had, but it inspired me. Once I knew how it felt, I would stop at nothing to keep it from happening again.

I flourished in goal; everything else in my life suffered. Never a great student, I moved into middle school and began skipping classes to stay home and practice, or watch reruns of NASL games on cable TV – a fantastic new reality. My grades plummeted. I spent all my time reading books about the World Cup, the great players -- Cruyff, Best, Banks, Eusebio, Beckenbauer -- and the great teams -- Manchester United, Bayern Munich, Real Madrid, River Plate. I learned world geography through soccer, knew exactly where Belgrade, Lisbon, Buenos Aires, and Milan were. I mowed lawns, saved money, and ordered my first real goalkeeper gloves from the Uhlsport catalog. Uhlsport, the brand of gloves worn by all the best pros. I had to wait several weeks for them to arrive. They had bright yellow latex palms and smelled wonderful. I wore them in bed and dreamed of one day playing in goal for the Rowdies.

My first hero was Winston DuBose, the Rowdies' keeper. He was young, American, and acrobatic, with a wild tangle of rock star hair. I had it all figured out: I was 14, Winston 23. He'd stay the number one for another seven or eight years, at which point he would turn the job over to me, and I would take it from there.

The first big proving ground was high school. I played for two years, growing and improving steadily. It became clear that I wasn't going to be very big by goalkeeper standards. At 18, I was a shade under six feet tall, and 130 pounds on a good day. But I'd been gifted with natural agility and reflexes, and like most young keepers, had a flair for the acrobatic. It drew attention. Nobody from my county had ever been offered a university scholarship, but I had my choice of a few when I graduated, with average grades, from high school. I chose Radford University in Virginia.

Not much went right at Radford. The NASL faded and died soon after I arrived, which caused me to rethink my goals. I decided I wanted to be the first American to play in England's First Division. It's all I thought about, when I should have been concentrating on academics and playing well for Radford. Instead, my performances were inconsistent: world beater one game, liability the next. My insecurity manifested in a sudden, terrible temper, and I quickly got a reputation for blaming every goal on my teammates, often at the top of my lungs. It's an act which grew old quickly, as some of the older players made clear. I tried to change, but it didn't matter. After two and a half years, my grades were so bad that my scholarship was rescinded, and in the spring of 1987, I was kicked out of school.

2

My back four tries to hold a high line and catch the opposition offside, but it doesn't work. The ball is played into the channel between my left back and a central defender, and they both give chase. "Stay Six, Stay!" I shout, hoping Matt Six, the central defender, won't vacate the space in front of goal. But he does, and neither he nor the left back can stop the speedy winger from hooking the ball across the face of goal, about eight yards out.

In my peripheral vision I see a flash of red, a striker running at full pelt to hit it first time. And in this moment, as it sometimes does, time seems to slow and my body becomes almost weightless, crackling with adrenalin. The shot comes, a flush half-volley, high to my right, where I'm already moving. I fling myself, twisting and reaching high and behind my body line, to claw it over the bar with both hands, before landing on the cool, green turf with a light thump. The striker holds his head in both hands; Matt Six claps me a couple of times on the shoulder and helps me to my feet.

I can remember every save of this sort I've ever made, the ones that really should have been goals. Frequently I remember, in addition to the save itself, small, irrelevant details that are not connected to the game. Tonight, as I wait for the corner to be taken, I notice that the top of the Empire State Building is swaddled in low, gauzy clouds. Winter is coming.

The corner comes over; Matt Six heads it clear. Play goes up the other end. We are not in a stadium, and there are no fans. I am playing for the Brooklyn Gunners, an

Chapter 2

amateur team, at Pier 40 in New York City. Most of the players in the league are in their twenties or early thirties. I am forty-five years old.

3

Back in Florida for the summer of 1987, a college flameout with no job, I had just one glimmer of hope: the Orlando Lions. Looking to fill a void after the demise of the NASL, the Lions, a collection of the best college and ex-pro players in the area, played friendlies against European professional teams on preseason tours, drawing surprisingly large crowds thanks to some slick marketing. The previous year, when I had still been at Radford, they had played the likes of Hamburg FC and Dundee United. Just before I returned to my last, ill-fated year at Radford, I trained with them a couple of times, after a friend who worked in their marketing department recommended me to Mark Dillon, the manager. I must have impressed Mark, because after just two training sessions, he put me in goal for their final game, against Catolica University of Argentina, and I played well in a 3-0 win. He told me to stay in touch, but I was still expecting to somehow make it to England, to be the first American to play in Division 1, so I hadn't thought much about them for the next year.

But with no team to play for after leaving Radford, I contacted Mark again, and he invited me to training at the start of the 1987 summer season. My first session went well enough, but as I begin training regularly, I realized with slowly mounting disquiet that I was in over my head. This had never happened to me. Though I underperformed at Radford, I was more than capable of playing well, and was as talented as anyone else. But the Orlando players were at a different level. An even split between Yanks and Brits, with a couple of Scandinavians thrown in, they played the game faster, smarter, and far more intensely than I had experienced before. They shot harder and more accurately, challenged me for crosses, demanded better distribution. They were impatient with my mistakes, and resisted my needy attempts to ingratiate myself. They approached the game like a job; they were there to work.

It didn't help that all the free equipment I'd received over the years at Radford had worn out, and I was stuck training in boots that were splitting at the seams and a pair of cheap, no-name brand gloves with almost no grip. The latex was so firm and slick that I slashed lines in the palms with a razor in hopes of improving the friction. It didn't work, but I didn't have the money for a decent pair.

The root of my problem with the Lions was that I couldn't get over the feeling of being an outsider. While I had toiled away at Radford, most of them played with and against each other at Central Florida, Rollins, Flagler, and other local schools. They had a shared history, with inside jokes and references I didn't understand. Instead of concentrating on playing well, I let it distract me, and spent too much time trying to make friends. I had yet to learn the first lesson of every dressing room in the world: you have to prove you can play before anybody will be your friend.

As the start of the season approached, I was still the only goalkeeper at training. But I knew I wouldn't be playing in the first team, because the Lions' first-team goalkeeper was none other than Winston DuBose, my boyhood hero. I couldn't wait to meet him, and looked forward to watching him from the bench, learning as his understudy. Just knowing that I would be playing with – or at least watching - my hero made me feel as if I'd made it; yet at the same time, it made me feel like a fraud. I knew I hadn't done anything to deserve it.

Winston wasn't due to arrive in town until the day of the season opener. He still lived in Tampa and had been training there with a local team. We trained on the afternoon of the first game, just a light session to warm the legs and let the players get accustomed to the Citrus Bowl's pitch. I arrived early, finding only one other player in the dressing room: Winston. I was only twenty years old, had never met a famous (to me) athlete, let alone one of my heroes, so I froze up a little, before stammering an introduction. He shook my hand and said, "Winnie."

Other players and club personnel began arriving, and soon we were out on the pitch in the cavernous stadium, bright summer sunshine streaming down on us. Winston went in goal for a few shots. Without even a decent warmup, he turned the first shot, a fizzing low missile, onto the post with his right hand. Amazing reflexes. He was on his feet instantly, gesturing for another shot. Guys lined up to shoot. The other Lions players didn't idolize Winston as I did, but they knew who he was and what he'd done in the game, and they were eager to see for themselves how good he was. Eventually, Mark sent me and a few others down to the opposite goal for some shooting. I kept one eye on Winston in-between shots.

After thirty minutes Mark sent us back inside, but Winston wanted to stay out and do some kicking - with me. It was my first chance to chat with him. I told him I was a Rowdies fan, that I could remember some of his best saves. He seemed pleased, but he wasn't easy to talk to. He was bristling with energy and didn't seem able to focus on just one thing. As we talked, he fiddled with his boots, his gloves. He made me nervous, and I began to babble. He indulged it for a while, then cut it short by saying, "Let's get some work done."

Chapter 3

We had one ball. He wanted to kick across the pitch, so he went to one side and I went to the other. He half-volleyed one right to me, and I struck one back at him, desperate to impress. We kicked back and forth for fifteen minutes, and my kicking, sometimes erratic, for once measured up. He said "Yes" or "Nice one" every now and then, after particularly good strikes, then signaled an end to the session. Walking back into the bowels of the stadium, he said, "Well, at least you can kick." Winston, I would come to learn, was generous in spirit but stingy with praise.

We had a pregame meal at the team hotel, another new luxury for me: the Lions pair up the players and give us hotel rooms on the day of games, so that everyone can be together and rest. It seems a wild extravagance – who's paying for this? - but as we have players coming from Tampa, like Winston, and Merritt Island, like me, it makes perfect sense. We would otherwise have nowhere to kill the six hours between the short training session and the 7:30 kickoff. Other guests eyed us curiously as we stood around in the lobby waiting for our keys, a large group of athletes exuding the rude health of youth. I felt a surge of self-importance as I caught them looking at us.

We napped the blistering afternoon away, and then gathered in the lobby to travel to the Citrus Bowl. We were playing, of all teams, the Tampa Bay Rowdies. They were not, of course, the 'real' Rowdies. Gone were the names and faces from the NASL days, replaced by young college kids or professional indoor players. But they were still a big name and a decent draw, and as we dressed, I could hear fans mingling outside and in the seats above us. I was the first to finish getting kitted up, and Ajit Korgaokar, an English defender, asked if I wanted a few shots. We walked down the tunnel and emerged into a completely different stadium than the one we trained in that afternoon. It was

still warm but the sun was setting, so the glare and
suffocating heat were replaced by a pink sky and soft, warm
breeze. Brilliant artificial light streamed from the looming
banks of floodlights. Most importantly, there was a crowd.
Not a big one, probably 5,000 people in a 50,000 seat
stadium, but they were all seated down low, right along the
touchline and around the tunnel from which we emerged. It
took both Ajit and me by surprise. We were the first players
they saw, and they broke into warm applause. Kids leaned
over the retaining wall and asked for autographs, then
cheered every time Ajit scored or I made a good save.

I had played in front of crowds at Radford: a few
hundred here, a thousand or so there, but never in a real
stadium. And they weren't adoring kids, like here. They
were often hostile, drunk college students, out for an
afternoon of abusive shouting and swearing. Adoring kids
are a lot better.

Ajit and I soaked up their attention as more players
from both teams trailed out of the tunnel. Winston finally
arrived, putting an end to my moment of glory, but he let
me help him warm up, hitting easy shots from the top of
the box. I watched from the bench as he turned in a
commanding, mature performance in a 2-0 win. His shot
stopping and handling was impressive, naturally. But what
caught my attention was the way he came for crosses,
directed and organized his back four, and distributed
intelligently. He had an obvious presence that everyone on
both teams could see. He was a real professional. It was a
keen and painful reminder of how much I still had to learn,
how far I had to go.

The glow from the pregame applause and attention
lasted throughout the game, and was augmented when kids
rushed the pitch for autographs after the final whistle. More
than I would have expected approached me. They knew my

name. The Lions had a smart, professional-looking program printed up, with a team photo and individual bios with head shots. The kids wanted me to sign under my face, and I obliged. At the same time Winston's performance highlighted how far I still had to go, signing autographs made me feel like I was a big star, just like him. It was a contradictory and confusing duality. For the moment, I chose to enjoy the attention.

Everyone was happy in the dressing room. The Lions were sponsored by Texas Light, a nonalcoholic beer. Cans sat on ice, untouched. As I would learn, the Lions, like virtually every team in the 80s, were not nonalcoholic beer types. There was a post-game party for players and fans at a touristy bar/restaurant in downtown Orlando. I showered and dressed quickly, knowing my mother was waiting for me in the parking lot, and we drove to the party together. The restaurant was crowded when we walked in, and I wondered if I was in the right place -- until some fans noticed me, and within seconds, everyone rose to their feet and applauded. This was a little too much, too embarrassing. I didn't play, after all, just sat on the bench, but they stood and clapped. I blushed and smiled and shook a few hands, signed a few more autographs. I loved the attention when I was on the pitch with Ajit, but it felt wrong here, genuinely disturbing, and I was relieved when the rest of the team showed up a few minutes later.

Winston warmed up to me a little bit, sitting at a table with my mother and me. He was alternatively thoughtful and manic, rushing off to share a joke at the bar, returning to deliver a considered take on the demise of the NASL. Fans hovered, but thankfully, the rock star treatment abated. I got a chance to socialize with my teammates for the first time. There was Ajit, and two other Englishmen: Ian Gill, an old adversary and friend from

Cocoa Beach High School, and Michael Riley, a short, stocky striker who, I would soon learn, will go out of his way to get a laugh at my expense. Oyvind Klausen, a commanding Norwegian midfielder, will also be hard on me. Rony Francois, from Haiti, will come close to breaking my fingers with the hardest shots I've ever seen.

And Mark Dillon, my first real manager. Mark was a true football man. He left the U.S. for Wales after college to play for Rhyl, a semi-pro team. He followed the game obsessively, knew every player on every big team in the world. I'd never met anyone else like that. He had built the Lions himself, from nothing more than a dream to reality in less than a year. It was easy to see that I could learn a lot from him.

It was a memorable but vaguely upsetting night. The attention from fans felt incredible, like a powerful feel-good drug; yet it was also embarrassing and undeserved, as I was only on the bench; and seeing Winston play in person sowed deep seeds of doubt in my mind. I was nowhere near that good. Would I ever be that good?

I hardly slept. The next morning, I stood bleary-eyed in my paid-for hotel room and watched a blood-red sun rise over the Orlando skyline. I had dreamed of nothing other than being a professional footballer since I was 12. I had never doubted it would happen. Until that morning.

Winston returned to Tampa after breakfast, not to be seen until the next weekend's game, so once again I was the only keeper in training all week. This was my chance to learn from Mark, to take my game up a level, prove myself to my teammates, but it went wrong from the start. I was on edge in training games, afraid to make mistakes but also too eager to impress; a terrible combination. I was tentative, slow to make decisions, yet also rash. I came for crosses too late or not at all, and held the ball for ages, unsure of how to distribute when I did manage to claim it. I was far too quiet.

Worst of all was that I was keenly aware of my failings even as they occurred, and kept desperately trying to make amends. This only caused further stress, more mistakes, more self-recrimination. It was a nightmare, and my teammates noticed. Oh, did they notice.

Lou Karbinier, a defender who played for the U.S. Olympic Team, scolded me several times for failing to communicate. Oyvind Klausen shouted his disapproval at almost everything I did. Michael Riley, meanwhile, minded his own business while we trained, but before and after sessions, he teased and needled me, a fake smile masking something I feared wasn't so benign.

Every dressing room in the world has a player who is like a shark that smells blood, a junkyard dog who senses fear. Dressing rooms are jungles, and you have to give as good as you get. Some players are too quiet, too loud, too cocky, too sensitive. My crime was neediness. I respected the Lions players and wanted them to like me, but I didn't let it happen naturally. Instead of training hard, keeping my mouth shut, and letting my ability speak for itself, I tried to ingratiate myself with each clique, especially the English players. I tried to demonstrate my knowledge of the English game, gleaned from reading stacks of books and *Shoot!* Magazine. Michael listened with a sardonic grin each time, before finally dismissing me with a curt, "What do you know about it, anyway?" I tried to laugh it off, but he wasn't joking.

There was Michael's way of doing things, and any variance was met with mockery. I wore smaller shin pads than he did -- he mocked me. I wore my hair longer -- he mocked me. I played golf one day, got a ridiculous tan line at my shirt sleeves, and he mocked me. Training became a chore. Every day as I drove to Orlando, I felt dread in my gut when I thought of Michael. It was obvious he hated me and he'd decided to make my life miserable.

He hadn't, of course. Ajit, his good friend, was a softer touch, and once or twice he advised me to laugh it off, that Michael didn't mean any harm. All Michael was doing was testing me, seeing how far he could go before I stood up for myself. It finally happened after we played the Rowdies in the return game in Tampa. He made fun of my sport coat at the after-game party, saying it was as thin as a bed sheet, and I agreed. "See?" he said to Ajit. "Whatever you say, he agrees with you."

"Fuck off, Michael," I said. It just came out. I wouldn't have said it if I had thought about it. He tormented me, but I didn't particularly want to fight him. He was short, but burly and strong, while I was all stringy limbs and pointy joints. He would have killed me. But he didn't want to fight either. He just half smiled and nodded, actually said "Okay," and from that point on, he eased off the teasing. We didn't become friends, exactly, but he treated me better, exchanged hellos with me before training, even occasionally chatted with me about the goings-on in English football. I was still not playing very well, but the Lions, through Michael, had taught me a critical lesson about survival in football: you have to push back.

Winston continued to drive over from Tampa for the "real" matches on weekends. I continued to watch him play, then sign autographs and feel important afterward. We played midweek training games, which Mark allotted to me. The first few went reasonably well, but then we played Rollins College on a Wednesday night. We won 1-0, which sounds good. But it was the shakiest clean sheet in history.

Chapter 3

My judgment was a disaster and my handling awful. The ball bounced all over my six-yard-box for ninety minutes, but somehow didn't go in. Mark looked at me askance in the dressing room but didn't say anything. I knew I played poorly and had been fortunate, but instead of seeing it as a reprieve, I dwelled on it.

All the while, I was working a minimum-wage day job at a resort in Cocoa Beach, and whatever money was left at the end of each week went into my gas tank for the 70-mile round trips to training. My boots were on the verge of death, the studs worn down and the seams almost completely split now. My cheap mystery brand gloves became more a hindrance than help. Back in my university days, Radford had supplied me with the highest-end Uhlsport gloves. Premium gloves feels wonderful on the hand. They have bulk, the solidity of quality German construction, and of course, they grip the hell out of a ball. But they don't last long, and by the time I joined the Lions, my final pair had worn out. It's true that gloves can't make saves for you, but a bad pair can certainly dent your confidence, and my confidence didn't need any more dents.

The Tuesday after the Rollins game, we played a semi-pro team from the Caribbean. They weren't great, but they played a direct, physical style, and had two giants up front. I was nervous before the game, as always, but also fearful. I knew Mark now had doubts about me. I knew he wouldn't keep me around forever if I didn't prove myself.

Right from the start, it went wrong, horribly wrong. They had a long throw-in specialist, and he chucked one in from my right. Be aggressive, I thought. Your ball. I called for it loudly, then realized in horror it was falling far short of my six-yard box. My defenders didn't challenge for it, having heard my call. I raced to beat their giant striker to it, but he got there first. I was far out of my goal, and he simply flicked it over me. I turned and watched it roll languidly into the empty net. A self-protective filter of some kind seemed to slide over my senses. I saw Lou Karbinier and Oyvind shouting at me, but it was like they were in slow-motion, and I couldn't hear what they were saying. It was hot, as always. The sun was still high despite the late afternoon hour, the Bermuda grass a brilliant green, lush with growth and health in the humid Florida summer. The ball sat nestled in the net, people were screaming at me, and I was pretty sure this was the worst I'd ever felt on a pitch.

Understand that prior to joining the Lions, I had been something of a star in the small soccer community in Florida. I had been an All-State player in high school, had earned a scholarship to a Division One university. I was used to feeling special on the pitch. There had been some tough times, of course - games lost, crosses misplayed - but I had never before been humiliated, as I was then.

We kept the ball for the rest of the game, so there was no chance to atone for my mistake with a spectacular save, no shot at redemption. Worse, we failed to score, so the ridiculous goal I conceded lost the game. The Lions did not take losing lightly, not even midweek training games; coming off the pitch, there were grumblings and curses and a few angry looks directed my way. But despite the game being over, I made still another mistake. The Lions went to Bluebeard's, a dive bar on Orange Blossom Trail, after every training session and game. But instead of holding up my hand and apologizing for my mistake, then joining the team for a beer, I simply fled the scene and drove alone back to Cocoa Beach, beating myself up the whole way.

This was what Mark Dillon took issue with at the next training session. "You're on thin ice," he told me. I have to start playing better immediately. And I can't run from bad performances. He told me that I should have been at Bluebeard's with everyone else, that nobody would ever respect me if I ran from my mistakes. We had another game coming up the following day, Thursday, against the University of Central Florida. "Your last chance," he said.

It was as if the worst had already happened: Mark was disappointed in me, and my teammates didn't trust or believe in me. So in a funny sort of way, despite it being my "last chance" I felt like the pressure was off. It couldn't get any worse, could it? I didn't dread the game. I barely gave it a thought. Of course it would be a disaster, but at least then it would all be over. I could go home, forget about being a professional footballer, quit the game entirely. When game time came, I was calm, but not in what would normally be a good way. I was resigned to failure, and eager to be done with it.

We played at our training pitch, site of so many of my recent follies, with the bulk of the Citrus Bowl looming against the skyline. It was a constant reminder: I play here, on this pitch surrounded by a chain link fence, and Winston plays over there, where it matters, inside a stadium that reached for the sky. I fumbled a few shots in warmup and laughed, certain I was the worst goalkeeper in the world.

The game started. UCF got a corner right away, and as it came swinging over, Mike Garvanian, one of our steely defenders, shouted, "Mike's ball!" But it was mine, plummeting right into the heart of the six-yard-box. As bad as things had gone lately when I'd shouted for the ball, I did it anyway. Mike, God bless him, got out of my way, I climbed high above him, stretched, and clasped the ball with my cheap gloves. The "thwack" sound it made as I caught it sent a feeling of goodness radiating through my body. I looked at the ball almost in surprise, unable to remember the last time I'd done something worthwhile in a game.

After a moment's reflection, I slung it out to Ajit. "Good boy," Mike said. Big moment.

Not much later, their left winger carried the ball at Ajit, cut inside him, and shot back across me from close range, to the near post. He must have thought he'd scored, but I flashed out a leg and turned it around the post for a corner. Ajit and Lou slapped me on the back, and even Oyvind nodded his approval.

I remembered some of the good games I had played for Radford, such as when we drew 1-1 with James Madison, or were beaten 1-0 by a John Harkes free kick against Virginia. I had faced a barrage of shots in those games, and made a number of spectacular saves. Despite goalkeeping being largely reactive, I felt in control, like nothing unusual or frightening was going to happen, or at least nothing I couldn't handle. That's how I began to feel, for the first time in a Lions shirt, against UCF. I played further off my line, communicated louder and better, kicked long and accurately. We scored in each half and won 2-0. In the dressing room afterward, Mark smiled his approval and said, "When the going gets tough, the tough get going." Never was I happier to hear a cliché. At Bluebeard's, I was a little more part of the in-crowd, not consigned to a corner with the kit man.

It didn't change everything. It was just one solid, competent game. But after weeks of shambolic training sessions and games, it felt like a watershed moment. At the very least, it kept me around.

Prior to one of the last competitive matches of the season, we had our usual light afternoon training session inside the Citrus Bowl, before heading back to the hotel. Winston surprised me by asking for ride. I'd picked his brain here and there throughout the season, but had never had more than a few minutes to speak with him, and he'd always seemed a little bit hesitant to embrace the role of mentor. Now, in my car, I gathered courage and forced myself to say, "I've had a tough summer. I feel like I'm making progress, but slowly. Any idea what I need to be working on?"

As it turned out, if you ask Winston DuBose what he thinks of you, you better be ready for the answer.

I'm not serious, he said. I'm not a goalkeeper; I'm just playing at being a goalkeeper. He'd been watching me. He said that when I was in goal for a shooting drill, I rested with my hands on my knees in between shots, "like a kid." He said that my kicking wasn't good enough, my communication wasn't positive enough, and that I wasn't strong enough. I stammered agreements, before remembering not to do that, and we drove for a few minutes in silence. Then his tone softened and he told me my form and technique were perfect, that my reflexes were impressive. He said I had plenty to work with, but he reminded me, again, that I needed to get serious.

I didn't know it was possible to be more serious about goalkeeping than I was. I thought about it all the time, just as I did when I was a kid. But Winston explained that real goalkeeping, serious goalkeeping, is not about spectacular saves. It's about positioning, footwork, communication, and distribution. "If you want a professional career, everyone you will be competing with can make saves. Making saves is the bare minimum requirement of the job. You separate yourself with the other stuff."

I had been fishing for a compliment, hoping he would tell me I had everything I needed and was on the right track. But his honesty was more helpful, and I began working harder to improve, concentrating more on communication in training, and staying late to work on my kicking on an empty pitch. But this newfound dedication did not extend to off-hours.

Drinking had, of course, been a part of university life at Radford, and I had joined in, but only because it was part of the overall experience of going out and trying to meet women. With the Lions, though, it was different. When we went to Bluebeard's, I drank for the sake of it, methodically and seriously, to get drunk. Back home, on days with no training, I drank with my friends. We were all newly of legal age and could drink in bars, but we found it too expensive, preferring instead to buy cheap beer and down it sitting on the hoods of our cars, parked on a new road still under construction. Between that and my sessions at Bluebeard's, I rarely went more than two consecutive nights without getting drunk. Thanks to my fast metabolism, I could drink a dozen beers with no recriminations the next day. But I wasn't getting enough sleep. I tried to make up for it at my job at a resort hotel on the beach, by sneaking into unoccupied rooms and sleeping. Finally, one evening, after almost nodding off as I stretched before training, I vowed to cut back. I went two nights without a beer, then three...

It didn't last. My drinking was pointless, really. It wasn't exactly "fun." We weren't out dancing with beautiful women in clubs, or relaxing in exotic beach bars. We were just a handful of idiots sitting on our cars in the dark, drinking the cheapest beer sold in Florida. We did stupid things -- climbed on the heavy road-building equipment left unattended, threw fireworks at each other. My drinking buddies weren't trying to be professional footballers. They weren't endangering their futures, just enjoying their youth.

Chapter 3

I, on the other hand, was being profoundly stupid, and on some level I knew it.

One night the crowd was thin, just my friend Chris and me, sitting in my car listening to the Dead Kennedys at a ridiculously high volume, emerging only to piss every thirty minutes. We were having a grand old time, just drinking, hardly speaking, when dazzling blue and red lights suddenly filled the world: police. Chris, who in point of fact had not yet turned twenty-one, frantically sprayed breath freshener in his mouth as the cop approached my window. We caught a break. The cop didn't care that we were drinking, just that we shouldn't have been parked out on a road not yet open to the public. He told us to head home, but not before saying, "Use some common sense, guys." It was mortifying. But it didn't curtail my drinking.

The last game of the season rolled around. We won again, and Winston played well again. I never got on the Citrus Bowl pitch all summer, but it didn't stop me soaking up attention from fans at the final post-game party. It was bittersweet: only mid-August, not even the end of the summer, but that was it for the Lions for another six months. We would continue to train and play the kind of midweek games that I played in all season, but I was already spoiled. I wanted games in stadiums under lights, in front of fans. In Orlando, when I stopped for a burger or to fill my car with gas, I half-expected people to recognize me. There are two million people in the Orlando metro area, and 5,000 of them at most went to Lions games. Yet I still hoped to be recognized.

It wasn't me who ran into a Lions fan, actually, but my mother. On her way to one of the games, she got lost in a residential neighborhood. Seeing a teenage boy in his front yard, she asked if he knew how to get to the Citrus Bowl. "Are you going to the Lions game?" he asked. When she told him "My son plays for the Lions," his eyes grew wide. When she told me this story, I played it cool, laughed it off, but was secretly delighted.

Early struggles with the Lions made me forget all about trying to get to England. It was hard enough keeping my head above water in Orlando. But as the season closed, I was feeling better about the way I was playing. I'd learned -- from Mark, from Winston, and from the psychological beatings I'd taken. I mentioned to Mark that I wanted to go to England to find a team to train with. His eyes lit up. "It's the best thing you can do," he agreed. "You'll learn to take crosses, to kick, to communicate. Great idea."

Mark said he knew someone who knew someone. He made a few phone calls. One day he told me it was all sorted. "You're going to train with Borehamwood F.C.," he beamed. I'd never heard of them. I knew Winston had done this sort of thing, gone to a Non-League club, in his early years with the Rowdies. He credited it with much of his education as a footballer. There was no question about it; I was going.

Of course, I had no money. Mark did what he could, by lining up clinics where I pocketed $50 for an hour or two of coaching. My actual job at the resort hotel kept me in gas and beer money, but not much else. Sensibly, I cut back on the drinking a bit, and began recruiting my friend Keith Ames, a promising player a few years my junior, to train with me in the early afternoons. He fired shot after shot at me, whipped in crosses for me to take, chased down my goal kicks. In our sessions, I felt like a completely new player. My handling was crisp and clean, my footwork sharp. I knew why: I felt vulnerable at Lions training sessions, but away from them, my insecurity vanished. It occurred to me that confidence need not be situational, that I could be confident no matter who was

Chapter 3

around. By the time I saved enough money to buy a plane ticket to London, I felt better about myself as a player than I ever had.

4

I had been to England once before, as a 16-year-old with my friend Colin, who had moved to the U.S. from England the previous year. As the home of football, I treated it like holy ground. It was summer, shortly after World Cup '82, so we couldn't go to any games, but I bought stacks of football books, magazines, and goalkeeper gloves, quickly exhausting my modest savings. It was a vacation, nothing but fun, and I had a guide in Colin who knew the territory.

This time, as my plane descended through cloud and fog over Heathrow, uncertainties awaited. I had a temporary place to stay, with friends of friends, but needed to find more permanent lodging almost immediately. I'd spoken to Borehamwood manager John Drabwell on the phone a couple of times, and while friendly, he seemed dubious about the whole enterprise. Eschewing even the pretense of tact, he once asked me if I was any good. "Can you play? I mean, do you know what you're doing?"

"I don't think I can prove that over the phone," I said.

"Well, we'll find out."

We didn't have long to wait; John put me through a training session on the day I arrived. I phoned him when I got in, exhausted from the eight-hour flight, just to let him know I'd actually gone through with it. He said, "Perfect, we have training in an hour. I'll come pick you up myself." Rain pelted down – it was early February, cold and dark -- so training was indoors, at a public gymnasium. John introduced me to the team. I just nodded and said hi,

Chapter 4

determined from the outset to not fall into the trap of trying to make friends. I didn't even know how long I'd be there. A week, a month, six months? It depended on how I did.

I wasn't bad that first session. Indoor five-a-side games highlighted my strengths, which were reflexes and handling, and masked my weaknesses, which were crosses, distribution, positioning -- basically everything else. John watched me closely. We played for an hour and I made a lot of saves, but he was perceptive, and picked up on one detail. "Low to his left," he said to his players during a shooting drill. "That's his weak spot."

He was right. Like most goalkeepers, I had a preferred diving side. Diving to my right felt natural, to my left somewhat labored and mechanical. Especially when a shot was low, I had a difficult time extending completely and getting a strong enough hand on it to keep it out. I didn't like that John -- 'Drabs' -- noticed this, but I respected it. It made me think highly of him as a football man. He didn't particularly look the part. Mark Dillon still looked like a footballer, but Drabs was a bit pear-shaped and wore bottle-thick, old-fashioned glasses. He was energetic, though, buzzing around the gym, peppering the players with advice and exhortations, occasionally bursting into streams of obscenities. When I finally got to sleep, I was pleased. I felt like I would be able to learn and improve there.

Two days later I took in my first Borehamwood game, and it was sobering. While the Lions played in the massive Citrus Bowl, Borehamwood toiled in a shambles of a ground called Broughinge Road. Covered on one side, the "main" stand seated about three hundred. There was open concrete terracing, no more than five feet high, behind each goal, and covered terracing of the same height running the length of the opposite touchline. Weeds sprouted from cracks in the concrete. There were no more than two hundred people in attendance, mostly in the main stand but also sprinkled around the terraces in pockets of twos and threes. The pitch itself was mostly mud. It was all romantically grim, until the game began, when it turned horrific.

The Lions played a patient possession game, but both teams on the pitch at Broughinge Road appeared interested only in kicking each other to death. Violent, chopping tackles flew in from both sides, but nobody seemed bothered. The pace was hypersonic, the ball played forward at every opportunity. Every now and then there was a moment of skill or composure, but for the most part, it was a street fight.

Ostensibly I was at Borehamwood to train and improve, but my competitive instincts kicked in immediately upon my first training session. The first team goalkeeper, Tony Tilbrook, wasn't there, but I got a good look at him that day, and he was mightily impressive. Though under six feet tall, he nonetheless dominated his box, knifing through crowds to pluck crosses from the heads of strikers. He kicked nearly the length of the pitch, both from his hands and the ground, and acrobatically turned away one shot after another, his form and technique perfect, before the game ended 1-1.

It was discouraging, and I was awake most of the night thinking about it. My concern wasn't that Tony was so good I'd never get to play for Borehamwood; it was that Tony was so good and yet only played for Borehamwood, in front of two hundred fans and for probably thirty pounds a week. How was this possible? How good must the goalkeepers be at all the league clubs, the fulltime pros? Even when I doubted myself the most, in my early days with the Lions, I felt it was just a matter of adjusting to a new level. I knew eventually I would hit a point where my talent would not be enough, but had hoped it would be much farther up the pyramid of the professional game. Had I found it that day, in the gray, violent drudgery of the Vauxhall-Opel League?

I was eager to impress and improve in training sessions, but I quickly learned yet another harsh lesson of Non-League football: there isn't much training. The players aren't fulltime professionals. They have day jobs. So training is taken twice a week in the evenings, and because at Borehamwood the groundsman didn't want anyone on the pitch, it consisted of little more than fitness runs. For my first session, we took to the dark, rain-slicked streets for an hour. The next session was the same. When the pitch was wet, we didn't train on it. I began closely observing the weather. We finally trained for real the following week, when the skies briefly cleared. Tony Tilbrook and I worked together at one end of the pitch. He was friendly, not at all threatened by my presence. He fired vicious shots at me from twenty yards with no apparent effort. I told him I wanted to strike a ball like he did. "It's all in the ankle," he said. "Keep it locked and strike straight through the ball like it's not even there." He looked down the pitch at the rest of the team, then back at me. "I'm not being arrogant, but I strike a ball better than any of them. I should give lessons."

Tony gave me the lowdown on life at Borehamwood. He laughed about the fans, said it was the same two hundred "grumpy old men" at every game. He said John Drabwell was a good football man but that he had it in for him, said Drabs blamed him for every goal. "He'll replace me with you first chance he gets," Tony said matter-of-factly, with no apparent bitterness.

With evening training twice a week, and two games a week, midweek and on Saturday, I was left with a lot of time to kill. Because I had very little pocket money, what I mostly did was take the train into London city center and walk. I went into Soccer Scene on Carnaby Street almost daily, gazing in envy at the soft, luxurious top-end gloves from Reusch and Uhlsport that I couldn't afford. I was still getting by on just one pair, a short-lived brand called Cannonball. They were an upgrade from the generic gloves I wore with the Lions, but not by much. I became a regular at the National Portrait Gallery, not because I was an aesthete but because it was free. I spent a lot of time in bookstores, though not because of any burgeoning literary interests. I mostly read books about football and sports cars. I found out-of-the-way streets with cheap pizza and burgers. I went entire days without speaking to anyone, apart from a perfunctory "Hello" or "Thank you" to shop attendants when I bought a paper.

I found permanent lodging in a nice, two-story house on a tree-lined street in Borehamwood. I rented two upstairs rooms from John and Lorna, a conservative, middle-class couple who could not fathom why I came all the way from Florida to play, or attempt to play, for a team such as Borehamwood. "But they're useless," Lorna protested.

She wasn't entirely wrong. As the weeks passed, I trained, ran the streets, and watched games. There were players with ability, like Tony, obviously, who had been an apprentice professional at Spurs, as well as Paul Read and Andy Falconer, a massive pair of central defenders who won every header. Terry Shrieves in midfield had a refined touch and could split defenses with sharply angled passes. But for the most part, Borehamwood games were won or lost on graft and commitment. After the initial shock, I became accustomed to the meaty tackling, the constant shouts of "Let's fucking have it!" and "Get fucking stuck in" from the players in the dressing room just before kickoff. I became accustomed to the oddities, like tea at half time. These same players who screamed and tackled, spat and cursed for forty-five minutes, would then spend ten minutes sitting with legs crossed, sipping tea. Not good tea, like Lorna made for me at home, but a thin, insipid brew, barely above room temperature.

It was not long before I saw evidence of the friction Tony alluded to between him and Drabs. At halftime, the manager would often challenge the goalkeeper, wanting to know why he came for one cross and not another, for example, and Tony never backed down, insisting he made the correct decision. I asked other players about it and they just laughed and insisted the two got on just fine, that it was just Drabs's way. In the dugout during games, he was frequently more entertaining than the football. He maintained a steady stream of invective directed at the ref, delivered in the resigned manner of an exasperated headmaster. After a bad tackle: "Oh come on ref, would you want that done to you?" After offside given against us: "Don't punish us because you can't keep up with play." Offside not given against the opposition: "He was cherry picking!" For linesmen operating in front of our dugout he had nothing but withering contempt, merely muttering, "Come on, lino," at every perceived injustice. Yet for all that, he was an astute tactician, always able to spot the opposition's weaknesses within the first passages of a game. The shame was that his team didn't always have the ability to play to his ideals.

Early March brought no relief from winter. I waited for Tony at a Thursday night training session, but he didn't turn up. I could tell from Drabs's demeanor that it was an unexcused absence. We took a short road run and played a bit of five-a-side. Before I left, Drabs pulled me aside and told me to bring my kit to the home game Saturday.

He had threatened to drop Tony once or twice before, but they always made up. I mentioned this to Terry Shrieves in the club pub after training, but he shook his head. "Not this time. He's really angry. You'll play." I felt a flutter of nerves, but still doubted it would happen.

Saturday broke cold and damp, the sky the colour of graphite, but the rain held off and the wind did not howl, for once, but only nagged at the treetops. The twenty-minute walk from my house to the ground seemed to pass very slowly. The route took me through council housing, where frequently I was stared at by sullen, mean-looking teens. That day the streets were cold and empty.

At Broughinge Road, people treated me differently. Arriving players looked me in the eye, slapped me on the shoulder, wished me luck. The nerves began to build, but I wouldn't believe it until I heard it from Drabs. Then Tony arrived. I had mixed feelings, wanting to play, but fearing the worst if I did. Drabs pulled Tony into his office. There was no shouting; we would have heard it if there had been. The other players began kitting out, but I waited. They emerged a few minutes later.

"Tony and I have talked it out," Drabs said. "I'll be dropping him today for disciplinary reasons. Justin will play in goal today. He says he's ready." Everyone in the dressing room turned to look at me.

No, I never said that. I most definitely would not have said that, because I didn't believe it. I had no idea what awaited me in the coming ninety minutes, but that I'm ready for it was not something I felt at all sure about. For a start, a silly thing: I forgot my shinpads. Tony let me borrow his, but they fitted me differently, felt funny, wrong. My nerves made me hyper, and Tony, to his credit, recognized this. "Don't worry," he said. "The result doesn't matter. We can't win the league, no danger of relegation. Nobody will blame you if something goes wrong. They'll blame me."

He had a point, and it helped a little. He put on a tracksuit and we took to the pitch, where he warmed me up for twenty minutes. We were playing Leatherhead. I'd heard of them. They're one of those Non-League clubs with an FA Cup history: they beat Brighton once, reached the 4th round before losing to Leicester. I watched them at the other end of the pitch. Some of their players looked enormous. I could feel my fingertips trembling inside my gloves.

I had nerves before every game; I think every goalkeeper does. Sometimes it was worse than others. Before the first game of my second season at Radford, I was so nervous that I could hardly think. It made no sense. I had played reasonably well the previous season, so I knew I was capable of playing at that level. But for whatever reason, the nerves hit hard that day. I went on to play fairly well, though we lost.

Nerves are good, for the most part. When the fight-or-flight response kicked in, adrenalin flooded your limbs. Your senses were heightened, your focus sharpened, reflexes and strength enhanced. Because of this, I'd made saves in games that wouldn't have been possible in training. But nerves are only good within reason. If they kick in too hard, it can become debilitating. Instead of excitement and anticipation, you feel dread, begin imagining worst-case scenarios. Once the game starts, you're either paralyzed or hyper-charged, each one as likely to lead to mistakes as the other.

Tony finished warming me up. His stinging shots in the cold, wet air got me thinking about my form and technique, and helped temper the nerves. We retired to the dressing room. The ground, I noticed, was entirely empty throughout the warmup. I was fine with that. When it comes to my potential humiliation, the fewer people who could see it, the better. From inside, though, as kickoff approached, I could hear them arriving. We went through the routine, familiar now, of Drabs shouting at each of us to get stuck in, and players shouting it back at him and at each other, only this time I was involved. I looked sharp in my kit: a silver Uhlsport jersey, black shorts, black socks. Ready or not...

The buzzer went off and we went out the door, down the tunnel, and onto the soft pitch. Over the tannoy they announced the team. When my name was read there was a murmur of apprehension, followed by polite applause. I'd have to win them over.

For a few minutes after kickoff, I was disoriented. The speed of the game was almost too much to keep up with. We took a corner, immediately got hit on the break, seconds later headed the other way on a counter attack of our own. Then I was involved: their right winger got a step on my left back, but he was falling backwards as he crossed, so it floated rather than whipped in towards the far post. Keeper's ball. I backpedaled, felt bodies behind me, shouted for it, jumped - and it stuck in my gloves. The small crowd cheered, slightly out of proportion to what I'd just done, which was to claim a straightforward cross under minimal pressure. Sometimes low expectations offer the best opportunity to make a good impression.

Taking the cross buoyed me. A few minutes later, one of my defenders was short with a back pass. I could see it was going to be picked off by a striker. I was off my line in a flash to spread myself, and the shot hit me in the ribs and spun away to safety. So far, so good.

The game churned around ineffectually in midfield for a while, and we missed a chance or two, and then they broke, exchanged a few passes, and won a free kick in shooting position, right at the top of the box. I set my five-man wall to cover my left post and positioned myself to the right side of goal. Three Leatherhead players stood over the ball. One squared it a few yards, offsetting it from my wall, and another ran up and belted a left-footer high to my left. It was going in. Thankfully, there was no time to think, only react. I flung myself, reached high with my right hand, and turned it over the bar. It was as good a save as I'd made in a competitive match for a long time. When the ref blew for halftime a few minutes later, I felt like I was glowing.

The dressing room was uncomfortably warm. I drank my tea just like a real Non-League player, which I now was. Drabs was not pleased with how we were playing overall, but he beamed at me and said, "Well done, the keeper. He's picking them like coconuts, isn't he?" This stopped me dead. It was an almost verbatim passage from 'Goalkeepers Are Different', a novel by Brian Glanville that I read at least a dozen times as a schoolboy. I didn't know if Drabs had quoted it intentionally or not. While I considered this, the buzzer sounded, and we were off again.

The pace dropped distinctly in the second half. Leatherhead didn't have much to play for, either. The crowd grumbled as passes went astray. After twenty minutes, I dared to allow myself to think about keeping a clean sheet. And just like that: penalty.

Football commentators, writers, and pundits of every stripe have misinterpreted how goalkeepers feel about penalty kicks ever since media types took note of football.

Let me tell you how a keeper feels when a penalty is awarded: he feels excited. You can only be a hero when facing a penalty. The shooter is expected to score, so nobody will blame you if he does. There may be anger on the surface, as the keeper remonstrates with the ref, but that's mostly for show. This isn't true if it's a penalty in the final minutes of a critical game, of course, one with title or relegation implications, but for most others, it is.

It was true for me. I had already exceeded my own expectations, and certainly those of the crowd, when the Leatherhead player stepped up to take the spot kick. Saving it would only make my debut better, while being beaten wouldn't really lessen it. In the ultimate anticlimax though, the Leatherhead player - I know to this day his name was Marc Smelt, because I read it in the paper afterward - smashed it a mile high and wide.

Towards the end we scored from a corner, and then added another. There's nothing a goalkeeper loves more than a two-goal lead, except of course for a three-goal lead. Two is all I got, but it was enough. At the final whistle I acted nonchalantly, as if I hadn't spent half the night awake with my guts churning, wondering if I would make a fool of myself. I shook hands with the opposition keeper and a few others, and gave a wave to the "crowd" of two hundred, before trailing back into the dressing room. I half-expected to get a hero's welcome, but my teammates, in various stages of undress, acted as if they'd already forgotten the game.

In the club pub afterward, a reporter from the local paper talked to me for a long time. I'm not sure why he bothered, because he didn't use any of my quotes in the story that appeared the next day. I was also approached by a man I had noticed around the pub before. He looked and dressed like a football man, always in a tracksuit, and it turned out he was the manager of St. Albans City, another Non-League club one or two leagues higher up the pyramid. He told me he'd been impressed with my performance and potential, and asked if I had considered going for trials at league clubs. He had connections at Brentford, he said, currently in the Third Division, and promised he'd put me in touch with them.

It was a heady night. Drabs gave me the same pay packet as the other players, £25. I was living on loose change, so it was not an insignificant sum. It was also the first time I'd been paid to play. Drabs was all smiles, telling everyone who would listen that I did great and would get more games. Tony didn't hear this, but he seemed genuinely pleased for me, too, telling me that he thought the save from the free kick was "a really good one." When I finally made it home and stumbled into bed, I had time to reflect on the game. Thrust into a new situation, a new and very different style of play, I came through. I'd played a competitive match on English soil. Okay, not at the highest level, not even close. But I was there to improve, to take steps, and I had. It seemed like a long time had passed since those halting, error-strewn training sessions with the Lions.

And yet...

My kicking had been nowhere near as good as Tony's. I left my back four unaware once or twice, when I failed to warn them of danger that Tony would have effectively communicated. Maybe it was the perfectionism of Winston rubbing off on me, but these inadequacies nagged at me, gradually overtaking my sense of satisfaction. I didn't fall asleep for hours.

Early the next week, I got a call from Steve Perryman, the Brentford manager. I wasn't home for the call - he left a message with Lorna. I remembered Steve

Perryman, of course, from the stacks of Shoot! magazines I devoured as a kid. He captained Spurs for years, including the 'Ricky Villa' FA Cup Final at Wembley. He left the briefest of messages - turn up for training on Wednesday. I was to meet him at Griffin Park, Brentford's ground.

I was nervous but not intimidated as I arrived at Griffin Park. I'd learned from my experiences with first the Lions and then Borehamwood: I'm not here to make friends or fly the flag for my country; I'm here to impress. Unfortunately, I couldn't seem to find anyone. I'd been traveling with Borehamwood, watching matches at tiny Non-League grounds, so even modest Griffin Park felt like a looming coliseum with its four covered stands. I ducked my head inside door after door before finally finding a player lying mostly naked on a table, getting a massage. He saw my kit bag and said, "You here for a trial?" There was the tiniest trace of sneer in his voice. I nodded, not wanting my accent heard just yet, and he told me to wait outside for "the others."

Eventually more trialists arrived. There were about ten of us, and I realized that Brentford must do it this way on purpose, bring trialists in all together at once, as a group. They put us in a van and drove us to the training ground, which turned out to be a public park near Heathrow Airport. We changed in a small, dark building that reminded me of an abandoned primary school, none of us looking at or speaking to each other. Through a wall, we could hear the Brentford first team players getting ready, shouting and laughing with the carefree manner that comes naturally when you have a contract. I tried to work out if there was another keeper trialing. We were all kitted out and ready, but unsure if we were supposed to sit and wait for someone to get us, or go out to the pitch on our own. I decided to

Chapter 4

take the initiative, and when I walked out, the rest followed me. It felt like a good omen.

For the first hour, we trained apart from the first team players. Perryman led us through drills. There were two other keepers, it turned out. He set up cones as small goals and had players shooting at us from fifteen yards. It played to my strengths and I did well. I snuck glances at the other keepers; they weren't professional standard. Neither were most of the outfield players, most of whom wouldn't have been good enough to play for Borehamwood.

During a break, Perryman chatted with me. He said that I came well-recommended, that the St Albans manager who got me the trial told him I looked like "the real thing." It felt nice, but it also caused a flash of nerves to race through me. I'd taken the news of a trial with Brentford in my stride because, frankly, I figured nothing would come of it. Now here was Steve Perryman making it sound like they were actually taking me seriously. It should have been motivation, but for the rest of the session I started thinking too much, not playing instinctively but making decisions based on what I thought Steve Perryman would like to see me doing. It caused me to hesitate a couple of times when we joined the first-team players for small-sided games. Still, I did better than the other trialists. One by one, Perryman pulled them aside and spoke to them quietly. Then, long-faced, the kid would trudge back to the changing room, shoulders slumped, dreams extinguished.

I finished the session reasonably well. Perryman walked past me and said simply, "See you tomorrow." I understood it was a victory of sorts, that the other trialists had already been sent packing, but I wished I had made a slightly better first impression. On the train back home, I replayed the two hours over and over again: good start, then panic-induced hesitancy, followed by a good finish. I vowed to do better the next day.

The next day went much the same way: some good moments (Perryman noticed one particularly acrobatic stop and said, "Nice save, goalie!") and some not so good. It wasn't like the early days with the Lions, when I was a stumbling, hesitant mess, full of self-doubt. It was more a case of being too impatient, too anxious to show that I was good. In small-sided games, I tried the extravagant instead of the simple, tried to release players with clever distribution, only to see it picked off time and again. The Brentford players grumbled a bit, but nobody shouted or screamed. Of all the trialists who turned out the day before, I was the only one invited back.

The first team goalkeeper, Tony Oliver, was about my age. I didn't know anything about him other than that he was new. If there was another goalkeeper on the books, I hadn't seen him. I had a tremendous opportunity; Brentford clearly needed another goalkeeper. My commute from Borehamwood was lengthy, took well over an hour, and I had to change trains a couple of times. It gave me time to think about this.

The Brentford players were friendly, but the truth is I didn't know any of them, except for Andy Sinton, who would go on to QPR and eventually be capped for England. The rest were just faces. They were good, certainly better than the Borehamwood players, but not necessarily better than most of the Lions. They were surprisingly young and small, many of them still teenagers. For the first two days, I assumed I had been training with the reserves. Then Perryman delivered a rousing speech about needing the points against Brighton at the weekend, and I realised these guys were it. They're the first team. And they weren't that much better than I was.

Chapter 4

In theory, at least.

In reality, things started to go wrong after two weeks. The problem was that I became too satisfied, too comfortable. I thought about how my time in England had gone so far - successful debut for Borehamwood, trialing at Brentford - and it seemed enough to me. Somehow, despite wanting to be a professional more than anything, I felt my motivation subsiding. I tried to get it back, but it was like grabbing for raindrops in a storm. What I really wanted was just the feeling of being a professional, and I had that by being on trial.

While I was training by day with Brentford, life went on at Broughinge Road. Predictably, Tony Tilbrook and Drabs made up and were pals again, so I was back in street clothes, watching games from the stand. I didn't tell anyone at Borehamwood about what I was doing at Brentford; it would have felt like bragging, and with just one game played, I'd hardly earned it.

Watching Tony Tilbrook at close range continued to be a revelation. When the weather was decent, I stood behind his goal, often the only person there. He had amazing natural spring, the kind of coiled elasticity that can't be taught or trained. High balls into the box were no more difficult for him than they were for the new breed of 6'4" keepers rapidly beginning to populate the higher levels of the game. He dealt with wind, rain, mud, and an erratic back four, and did nothing less than make fantastic saves game after game. In the aftermath of my clean sheet debut, I gained a bit of status around the club – the pub regulars smiled and said hello, my teammates treated me more like one of them rather than a stranger who dropped in for a short time - but there was no more talk of me getting another game. Secretly, I was okay with that. My debut went so well that another game or two would only be anticlimactic, or possibly disastrous. In any case, I was focused on Brentford.

Except I wasn't. I continued to show up to training on time, train hard, and keep my mouth shut. But a player on trial has to do more than that. He has to make it impossible for the manager not to notice him. I should have been showing up early, staying late, and most importantly, playing with desperation and hunger rather than comfort. Try as I might, though, I just couldn't shake that feeling of comfort, as if I'd already achieved something just by being there. Subconsciously, I was thinking about the people I played with and against growing up in Central Florida, the guys at Radford, the Lions. Already I could say to them, "I kept a clean sheet on my Vauxhall League debut. I trained every day with a Football League club." There was so much more there for the taking, but I didn't take it.

After my third week of training, Steve Perryman pulled me aside and said, "To sign you, we'd have to think you're better than who we already have, and we don't." I had known this for some time, but it still stung when he said it. He invited me to continue training with them. He said it would help both parties - they needed another goalkeeper in training, and I would continue to stay fit and sharp. He also said that he might be able to help me - if he heard of another club in need of goalkeeping support , he would pass my name along.

I agreed, thanked him, and continued to train for another couple of weeks. But eventually I stopped going. What Perryman said was true - it could only help me to keep going. But I started to feel my time in England coming to an end. After almost four months, I was not homesick, but I did miss my friends and the Florida sun. There was still a month to go in Borehamwood's season when I told Drabs I was ready to head home. I felt a sense of relief and

Chapter 4

a little bit of pride that it was over. It went well. Could have been better - could have played more games for Borehamwood, given a better account of myself at Brentford - but I came to learn, and I felt like an entirely different goalkeeper than the one I had been when I arrived. Mission accomplished.

I returned to Florida's heat and sunshine in May 1988 and contacted Mark Dillon. He invited me to Lions training, but it was too late for me to win a first team spot (as I knew it would be when I went to England). The Lions had joined a new league, the unimaginatively named American Soccer League, and had already begun league play. The Rowdies had lured Winston back to Tampa, so the Lions signed a couple of American keepers close to my age.

I joined the Lions, who in addition to the keepers had several new faces, for a training session, relaxed but eager to show my improvement. John Higgins, Mark's number two, put the keepers and me through a torturous session, and I came through it well. Afterward, the Lions' new Public Relations Officer approached me. She wanted to hear about my time in England. I relayed the story and she said, "This is good, could be a good story." By the time I got home, she had left a message for me, saying that at training the next day, the local TV news channel would be there to do a report on me.

A special TV report about *moi*. This was not something I needed to be convinced to do. Training the next day, Friday, was in the Citrus Bowl, ahead of Saturday night's league game. The team went through a light session, and then the TV crew showed up. They interviewed Mark Dillon, who presumably said nice things about me, and then me. The reporter opened with a statement rather than a question, something like, "Well Justin, you traveled a long way to play soccer." I waited for him to ask an actual question, realised he wasn't going to, and did my best with the opening. We talked for two minutes, the questions getting easier and more direct. Some of the Lions' new players looked on, probably wondering who I was and why I was being interviewed.

The report aired that night. It was mostly good. I didn't look too skinny, which was my biggest concern, nor did I sound too dumb. My classic silver Uhlsport jersey looked terrific, and my answers weren't bad. The only gripe I had is that they decided my story needed an "angle," and the angle was my supposed determination. The reporter's voiceover said something about how I was so determined to make it as a pro that I went all the way to England to train. Then he asked Mark Dillon about my determination, and then me, and then more voiceover about determination as I was shown making a save. It ended with a clip of a shot beating me. Thanks for that.

I turned up for the game on Saturday, but it felt weird. I wasn't actually on the team, which only really occurred to me as I was standing around the dressing room as the players got kitted out. I wandered out onto the pitch and then, feeling out of place there, clambered up into the stands, which were mostly empty, an hour before kickoff. As a modest crowd filed in, a woman recognized me from the TV spot. We chatted for a minute and it was a nice ego boost, but I was eager for the game to begin, and even more eager for it to end. It was going to be a long summer. Mark wanted me to keep coming to training, but I didn't have anybody to play for, and I didn't have any money. I needed a job.

I was hired again at the beach resort where I had worked before going to England. It was an easy job, driving a golf cart around a lush, tropical compound, bringing newspapers and toiletries to guests. I worked from six in the morning until two in the afternoon. I'd never been an early riser, but the dawn starts were mitigated by the fact that I often slept on the job. I alone had a key to a closet full of rollaway beds, so after I raised the flag and delivered newspapers, with the sun breaking over the roaring waves of the Atlantic, I could often sleep for an hour or two. It was not a bad gig, but not how I wanted to spend the rest of my summer, let alone my life.

Predictably, I began training less and less frequently with the Lions. After finishing work at two, I rarely had the energy to make the hour-long drive into Orlando, and when I did, I felt like a third wheel. Three keepers meant one had to stand and watch during small-sided games; that one was me.

With little else to occupy my evenings, I slipped back into my hard-drinking habits. I was spared hangovers by my rapid metabolism, but as the summer rolled on, I trained less and less regularly. I didn't really miss it - perhaps I needed a break after coming back from England. I kept tabs on the Lions. They were doing okay, not bad but not great, in their inaugural ASL season. I stayed in touch with Mark Dillon and he gave me some work, a few days at the Lions' summer camp for kids, during which I somehow ended up on TV again, when a news crew visited for a human interest story and couldn't find anyone to talk to but me. But as July melted into August, it became clear that I needed a new plan.

Near the end of their season, the Lions were eliminated from playoff contention. Shortly thereafter, the team's ownership fired Mark Dillon. It was a shock. Even though I'd been on the outside looking in, Mark had kept in contact with me, kept me involved. He was pleased that I followed through on going to England and made good use of my time there. He told me several times that I remained in the Lions' long-term plans. But now he was gone. There would be a search for a new coach, but for the time being, John Higgins would run the show. This was good news: John, like Mark, considered me part of the Lions' family, even while not officially a member of the team.

My friend in the Lions' front office alerted me to a particularly intriguing piece of gossip: as his first order of business, John, she said, was planning to take the Lions on a tour of Scotland, and he wanted to take me along, on a professional contract, as one of two goalkeepers. The other being Winston DuBose. I cursed her, told her that if this didn't come to pass, I would never forgive her. But she was confident. "John asked me to let you know," she said. "He wants to make sure you're training. But you're not an officially contracted ASL player, so there may be some insurance concerns." She said John had put the question to the league and would have an answer soon.

I went into emergency training mode. Instead of rushing home to sleep, I ran on the beach after work. In the evenings I met up with Keith Ames, and he fired shot after shot at me, bent in crosses, chased down my goal kicks, just like he did before I went to Borehamwood. I cut way back on the drinking. At night I stared at the phone, willing it to ring. This chance had come from nowhere, but it offered a lifeline I could now taste. Professional contract, tour of Scotland. Winston. It had to happen.

John called. Still no word from the league, he said, but he wanted me to come to training in case. In addition to the familiar faces, John had invited a handful of players from other ASL teams. There was Winnie and Davey Powers from Tampa, Jeff Guinn from Albany, Troy 'Chopper' Edwards from Ft Lauderdale, and Michael Brady and John Kerr from Washington. The first training session was cracking - players trying to impress each other, the ball whizzing around - but at one point, I felt a twinge in my left hamstring. When I woke the next morning, I could straighten my leg only with difficulty. I wobbled around for two days, taking a break from extra training with Keith, and at the next Lions session, I couldn't hide it. I assured John I'd be fine, that it was just a twinge. "That's good," he said. Then he smiled but didn't say anything else, just looked at me. I smiled back, unsure of what was happening. "Come with me," he finally said.

Inside the Lions' offices at the Citrus Bowl, a secretary produced a multi-page contract. John showed me where to sign. It was a two-week tour, with games against Celtic, St. Mirren, Aberdeen, and Dunfermline Athletic. I'd be paid per game, $250 each, with a further $500 for expenses. $1500 total for two weeks. My job at the hotel paid less than $5 an hour, meaning I would do well to make $1500 in two months. The contract was only for the length of the tour, of course, just two weeks. The Lions would then be in a lengthy offseason, and all the players would need to find paying work of some kind. But do well in Scotland, John said, and there will be a place in the squad for me for the next ASL season; assuming he was given the job on a permanent basis.

My head spun a little, but instead of euphoria, my first reaction was concern. This can still go wrong, I thought. My hamstring was still troubling me, making all movement difficult and explosive goalkeeping painful. There were also logistical difficulties: we left for Scotland in ten days. There was no chance of getting all that time off work, which meant I would have to quit my job. That wouldn't win me any friends at the hotel, where in truth they'd been pretty good to me, but it had to be done. I phoned them right there from the Lions' office. No time like the present.

Chapter 5

We began training every day, and for the five days prior to leaving, the Lions put us up in a hotel near the Citrus Bowl. After one session, John handed us each an envelope. Inside were fifteen traveler's checks. $100 each. Signing the contract did not really make me feel like a professional, but this did! It sounds quaint now, but $1500 cash in hand in 1988 felt like a lot of money. I felt, frankly, rich.

It was great to be around Winston again. It had only been a year, but thanks to my time in England, I was a greatly improved goalkeeper, and he seemed to recognize it. We trained together in the stifling late-August heat, and he treated me more like an equal than an understudy. John told me that I would definitely play in some of the games, though he hinted that he may give Winston all ninety minutes against Celtic, the first match. Whilst I was, of course, elated at this sudden and amazing turn of events, I had familiar misgivings, fear about how I would play when called upon. Thus far, the best team I'd ever played against in a proper game was... Leatherhead. I may not play against Celtic, but I would be playing against Aberdeen, only five years removed from beating Bayern Munich and Real Madrid in the European Cup Winners' Cup. My apprehension was heightened by an inconvenient development: I had begun to feel claustrophobic in small, crowded spaces, including planes and buses. I had a lot of both in my immediate future.

Travel day. We flew ninety minutes from Orlando to Atlanta, then nine hours transatlantic to Glasgow, much of which I spent pacing near the rear of the plane when the seatbelt light was off. We arrived dazed and jet-lagged in the early evening. A minibus whisked us away from the airport and city center and deposited us at our home for the next ten days, Jordanhill College. The dormitories were empty,

the students still away for summer, and we commandeered
a building with a ground-floor lounge with a TV, over-
stuffed sofas, and a table tennis table. We collapsed onto
our beds – I shared a room with Steve Torkelson, Oyvind's
gregarious friend from Norway who joined the Lions the
previous season - and slept until late morning.

After breakfast, Oyvind, team captain, told us to
prepare for a short kickaround. Not a full training session,
just a light jog and stretch. I asked if I needed to bring my
gloves, and he said no. There was a pitch on site, lovely and
lush, but when John split us into two teams, it was clear he
planned more than a light kickaround. Winston was
annoyed that I'd left my gloves behind, despite being told to
do so by Oyvind. "Always bring your gloves!" he barked.
My face flushed.

This was how it was going to go for me, I thought. I
was finally a pro, or something like it, and I was going to
fuck it up on the very first day. We moved the goals closer
together to play eight versus eight, and Winston trotted
down to the far end of the pitch. John stood in the center
with a ball in one hand and a whistle in the other. The nine-
hour plane ride had freed us from the prison of Florida's
summer heat - great for the beach, no good at all for
football. The air was crisp, metallic, as if it was charged with
ions. I breathed deeply and felt all my negativity and doubt
flow away. John blew his whistle and dropped the ball into
the fray. Oyvind, playing for the other team, won it, strode
forward, and lashed it towards my left-hand post. I didn't
have time to think, only to react. I flung myself, turned it
around the post at full stretch with my bare fingertips, and
crumpled to the cool, soft turf. It turned out that *this* was
how it was going to go for me here.

That first session was tremendous, shots flying in
from everywhere, Winston and I trying to outdo each other.

Chapter 5

So much happened in my head in so little time: I realized that I was good at this. Not passably good, not acceptably good, but professionally good. Winston, of course, was better overall, but not by as much as I'd always assumed, and especially not as a pure shot stopper. Bare handed, I'm flying, plunging, diving, in an ecstatic joy that reminds me of how it used to feel in my backyard Dust Bowl. We played to the last goal, and my team got it, but only after I made a miracle save, rushing across my line to save a piledriver volley from my roommate Steve Torkelson. When we ended the session with a goal at the other end, my team celebrated as if we'd won the World Cup, and Winston howled in protest.

We dined together and then gathered at an on-campus pub, mostly empty since few students were around. We quickly took it over. We were loud and, based on the looks we got from the students, annoying. This was a lesson I hadn't yet learned about Britain: people love football much more than they love footballers. In the U.S. it was still an 'alternative' sport, played and appreciated by alternative and generally progressive people. But in the U.K., footballers were respected for their athletic prowess, perhaps, but not their brains, charm, or social graces. I saw it there, in the pub, but I didn't care, none of us did. The pub was ours. We drank lightly, played darts, played pool, but had an early night. We had training in the morning and then the Celtic game the day after.

We had another good training session the next day. Afterward, wanting a little alone time, I went into the city and found a sports shop, and indulged in a way I hadn't been able to in years. After trying on dozens, I chose a pair of Reusch Toni goalkeeper gloves. They were a lovely shade of light blue with purple accents on the backhand, with a pillowy soft white palm. I hadn't owned decent gloves since

I was at Radford. I stared at them on the entire bus ride back to Jordanhill.

Steve Torkelson and I spent the rest of the day playing table tennis. We met as a team with John after dinner. He gave the first eleven - Winston in goal, as expected - and for the first time there was a sense of pressure through the team. The games were just friendlies, of course, but for most of us they were more than that. It was a chance to test ourselves against established pros, in real football grounds, maybe even be noticed by scouts.

On Saturday morning, I got put through an 11th-hour wringer. Apparently Winston and Davey Powers had gone out for a late-night vindaloo curry, and it devastated Winnie's digestive system. He was up all night and not in any condition to play. But almost as soon as John told me this, Winnie, somewhat palefaced, reported that he was fine. I felt a mix of relief and disappointment, but mostly the latter. I wanted to play.

We took a bus through Glasgow to Celtic Park. Fans milled around outside the ground when we pulled up. They smiled tolerantly, even bemusedly, at us as we walked from the bus and through the front doors, to be greeted by a replica of the European Cup Celtic won in 1967. A club official gave us a quick tour of the reception area and trophy room, then took us below pitch level to our dressing room. In contrast to the plush carpeting and paneling upstairs, the dressing room was nothing special, just plain white walls and an unfinished cement floor. Once inside, we went very quiet. Nerves.

I dressed faster than anyone else. As I was likely the only one who wouldn't get to play, I at least wanted some time on the pitch, and arranged with Ajit to go out early for some shooting. He fiddled with his boots and I was

Chapter 5

impatient, so I grabbed a ball and went. A few Celtic officials standing in the tunnel smiled and nodded at me as I walked towards the dim sunlight. A few more steps and I was outside. Celtic fans leaned over both sides of the entrance to the tunnel. A few of them clapped politely. I tossed the ball onto the pitch, dribbled it out to midfield, then turned, taking in the stadium. It was enormous and dark, covered by a hulking roof. Three sides were completely empty, but the main stand, from under which I'd just emerged, was beginning to fill. I felt a swell of pride standing there, a twenty-two year-old American goalkeeper, on the cusp of what was obviously going to be a glorious professional career.

Ajit emerged from the tunnel and stepped onto the verdant pitch. I pinged a left-footer to him, but he looked away just before I struck it. It sailed past him, hit the advertising boards, and ramped into the crowd. A hundred kids jeered at me, an awful sound. So much for the cusp of a glorious professional career.

By the time we kicked off, 7,000 Celtic fans were in the ground, expecting an easy game. Celtic put out a reserve side, young players eager to make an impression. But to everyone's surprise, especially our own, we took a shock lead. Mark Lamb sprung an offside trap and coolly lobbed Alan Rough as the keeper came off his line. Much to the amusement of the crowd, we celebrated the goal as if we were insane. Celtic responded by not letting us have a touch for the rest of the half, forcing Winnie into a half-dozen brilliant saves before finishing twice. It was more of the same in the second half, though we managed a late consolation goal. The 4-2 final score flattered us, yet the Celtic crowd applauded us politely and John was reasonably pleased. Several of our players had run themselves to near-exhaustion.

We met and mingled with Celtic players and officials at a post-match reception. Winston told an official that he'd like to meet Pat Bonner, Celtic's Republic of Ireland goalkeeper currently out with a back injury. The official duly brought him over and the two of them chatted for a minute as I hovered nearby, eavesdropping. Bonner responded to Winnie's questions with short, unanimated answers before excusing himself. It angered me, but Winnie waved off my protestations. "The guy's injured, he's got other things on his mind."

We had a light training session on Sunday, ahead of Monday night's game at St. Mirren. John told me I would be playing the second half. He must have told Winston this as well, because he was quiet throughout the training session. When it ended, Winston told me to stay behind for extra training. He set up a few cones and started kicking balls at me without fully explaining what I was supposed to be doing. When I began tentatively, reaching for a ball with one hand, he exploded.

"What is this shit? What are you doing?" he shouted. "You're going to be in there tomorrow night, against full-time pros! Are you going to just stick out a hand, or are you going put out some effort?"

I stammered a response, said I didn't understand the drill, and he shook his head. "Start again," he said. I got through it and a few more drills in icy silence. After thirty minutes he muttered, "That's enough." We collected the balls and walked back up the hill towards the dorms. Outside the front door, he asked me to sit.

"Look," he said. "I'm not trying to give you a hard time. I just don't think you know what you're up against. These guys are going to be coming at you in waves, whipping in crosses, hammering shots. You've got to get your head on straight."

"I'm ready," I mumbled, starting to get defensive.

"You're *not* ready. This half-assed shit-" (he mimics me listlessly sticking out a hand) "-is not going to get it done."

"I just didn't understand the drill."

He looked at me for a moment, then nodded, seemingly satisfied. When he spoke again, his tone was softer. "You've got to decide if you're going to be a serious pro. We've got guys here complaining about the dorms, complaining about the weather, complaining about the food. They have no idea what an incredible opportunity this is."

"I'm not one of them, honestly. This is the best thing that's ever happened to me."

"John told me you haven't even played all summer? What the hell have you been doing? You have to be a year-round goalkeeper."

"I came back from England too late to make the team. I felt like going to England was more important."

"You've got a lot of balls for doing that. But it's not enough. Everything matters: the food you eat, the way you take care of your kit. Look," he said, pointing to my boots, covered with mud after training. "What's the first thing you're going to do when you go inside? Clean those boots."

I nodded. I knew he probably was not happy about splitting the next game with me. I considered saying something about it, but it seemed he'd made his point and had calmed down, and the last thing I wanted to do was rile him again. He patted me on the shoulder and walked inside.

Although I felt a little like a small child scolded for stealing a cookie, I knew that he only wanted me to improve. In any case, I didn't dwell on it long. I began thinking about what it would be like when I took to the pitch at Love Street the next night. Here come the nerves. The evening seemed to drag on forever, especially as we couldn't kill time with pints in the pub, and I didn't sleep well.

Steve Torkelson and I passed much of the next day playing table tennis. To Steve's credit, he could see I was nervous, so he didn't say anything about the match, just kept making me play game after game. It worked. I beat him several times, until he started serving with maddening spin, and I spent the afternoon trying to figure out a way to beat him. It prevented me from obsessing all day about the game. It's important to prepare and focus, but it does you no good at all to do so for hours and hours.

The sky was already darkening as the bus pulled up to Love Street. The stadium was bigger than I had expected, largely because of the vast roof above the main stand. Floodlight pylons towered above us. For six months, the pinnacle of my playing career had been my successful debut for Borehamwood, played in what could only very generously be described as a 'stadium' in front of two hundred people. As I looked at Love Street silhouetted against a late summer sky, I saw past nerves to opportunity: tonight I could author a new highlight.

As always, I got kitted out quickly, though with more attention to detail this time, knowing that I would be playing. I helped Winnie warm up. The pitch was lovely, green and sparkling under the floodlights after a brief misting from the sprinklers, but the stadium was empty. Perhaps St. Mirren fans couldn't be bothered to pay to see a strange American team on a Monday night. It was hard to blame them.

Chapter 5

We went back down the tunnel after warming up. In the dressing room, John went around to each player, quietly instructing and motivating, before delivering a speech to all of us. We lined up in the narrow tunnel next to the St. Mirren players, then walked out alongside them. I was last in line, so it came as a surprise when I emerged onto the pitch and saw much of the terracing on the far side filled. It was not a big stand, held maybe 4,000 under a low roof, but it looked and sounded like more. They welcomed us – or, more accurately, the home side - onto the pitch with a strong-throated series of chants, and now it felt very real.

Winston was busy almost immediately. We had a hard time tracking all the runs the St. Mirren players were making. They got in behind us twice, but Winnie stood up big and strong and kept them out. Their fullbacks overlapped with impunity and had ages to pick out their crosses, while at the other end, we were unable to hold the ball up and keep any meaningful possession. We withstood the barrage for thirty minutes before our resistance broke, and St. Mirren scored twice in rapid succession. Time for an ugly confession: I wasn't that disappointed when they scored. I was under enough self-imposed pressure as it was, having to take over from Winston. If we were already losing, there wasn't much I could do to make things worse.

At halftime, the players headed into the dressing room while I pulled on my new gloves. Winston walked with me down to the far goal to warm me up. Instead of starting me with a few easy shots to warm up my hands, he smashed a half-volley at me from ten yards out, then shook his head disdainfully when all I could do was turn it over the bar. After another dozen vicious shots, the players emerged from the tunnel again. Maybe Winston knew exactly what he was doing: dealing with his shots hadn't been the best physical preparation, but it took my mind off the game.

When we kicked off, I felt loose, relaxed, even strangely confident.

The fans in the terracing to my right kept up a steady stream of songs as St. Mirren probed for a way through. Happily, I didn't have long to wait for a touch. On my Borehamwood debut, I got my first touch after the opposition sent in the easiest possible cross to deal with. Amazingly, the same thing happened again: their right back overlapped, made space for a cross, and stood up a floated ball to the edge of my six-yard-box. The right back had been well ahead of the play, so there were no St. Mirren players arriving in the box to challenge as I rose and claimed it at full stretch. There is nothing like a successful first touch when you're nervous.

Soon after, I had a save to make, and it was a good one. This time it was the left back running free. He slipped a ball inside my right back, and a St. Mirren player ran onto it, twelve yards out and at an angle. The way he shaped his body to get it onto his right foot tipped me off that he was going to bend it around me to the far post, low to my left. I took a small step that way just as he shot, then dove, twisted, and held it as it smacked into my gloves. The crowd went *"Ooohhh!"* and then applauded me politely, and my teammates shouted their appreciation. I was practically glowing with positive energy. This is the positive side of nerves, the flood of adrenalin and euphoria you get when things are going well. I made another save or two, claimed another cross, and the game ended as it stood at halftime, 2-0. I pretended to be disappointed that we lost, but I was elated with how my night had gone.

"Smooth, very smooth," said Chopper to me in the dressing room. Oyvind patted me on the shoulder and John Higgins ruffled my hair. Everyone else compared the shirts they'd traded with the St. Mirren players. In my fog of

Chapter 5

satisfaction after the final whistle, I had neglected to find an opponent to trade with. When Winston realized this, he disappeared into the hallway. Two minutes later he returned with St. Mirren keeper Les Fridge's jersey and handed it to me. That was Winnie: gruff one moment, selfless and generous the next.

My debut had gone as well as I could have hoped for, and I was euphoric. But strangely, my instinct was to spend time alone, away from the rest of the players. It wasn't motivated by bad or negative feelings; I just felt like after a week of training and living together in Orlando, followed by another week in close quarters at Jordanhill, I'd seen enough of everyone else and they had seen enough of me. For the next two days, we trained in the morning and had the rest of the days and nights to ourselves. I spent mine wandering alone through Glasgow. There was a festival of some kind going on, with a small but fast roller coaster. I rode it a half-dozen times consecutively, racing back to the end of the short line after every ride. I lingered in bookstores, sports shops, and museums. It was like my days wandering London the previous winter, except that I had a little cash in my pocket, and was buoyed by a greatly enhanced self-image. It was ridiculous, but as I walked the streets, I wondered if any of the people I saw had been at the St. Mirren game. I recognized this persistent desire for validation as needy, but at the time, it seemed harmless.

On Wednesday morning, we piled into a large luxury bus and drove north all day to Aberdeen. We stopped for an hour at St. Andrews. I rented a putter and putted alone for twenty minutes on the public practice green of The Old Course. The tide was out, miles out, leaving a flat vista of charcoal sand beneath charcoal sky. Autumn had come already to the north. A cold, brooding wind raced across the empty bay. I shivered in my lightweight Lions tracksuit. I returned the putter and explored the narrow, Gothic streets that wound through the University of St. Andrews. In a small secondhand bookshop, I bought a well-worn copy of *The Woodlanders*, a Thomas Hardy novel I'd not yet read. For the rest of the drive to Aberdeen, I alternated between reading the book and taking in panoramas of the North Sea. Two or three times, I had to close my eyes and breathe deeply when I felt stirrings of claustrophobia.

We received a muted, formal welcome from officials of Aberdeen Football Club. They had made a slow start to their season, and were treating this as a competitive game, a chance to work out their technical and tactical problems, by sending out a strong squad filled with first-team players. Winnie was under immediate fire, mostly in the form of an aerial bombardment that he handled brilliantly. After the fourth or fifth cross he claimed, an Aberdeen coach shouted from the little dugout next to ours, "Keep them away from the keeper!" I imagine that's the ultimate compliment a goalkeeper can get from the opposition.

Much like in the St. Mirren game, we found ourselves getting pegged further and further back, and finally gave away a goal. Another quickly followed, and once again we were down two-nil at the half.

As Winnie pummeled half-volleys at me, I was slightly less nervous than I had been at Love Street. Pittodrie is an all-seater stadium, and the crowd, maybe 4,000, was confined to the main stand. As soon as we kicked off, the play buzzed around me, Aberdeen whipping the ball around us like we were standing still. I got down to the first shot, a hard, skipping one to my right, pushed it around the post, then punched away the corner under pressure. I frequently did not punch the ball well, but got good height and distance on that one. Another shot came in, right at me but low and skipping on the dewy turf. I smothered it and clutched it to my chest, my forehead against the damp grass, and felt the cold air burn my throat as I sucked in a breath of relief. A wave of polite applause from the crowd washed over me. It felt good, giving a good account of myself, in these stadiums, in front of these crowds, in front of the same guys – Oyvind, Ajit, Rony Francois – I struggled with so badly the previous year. It felt so good it was almost narcotic.

It didn't last for long, though. A quick one-two at the top of the box, a swing of the right boot by John Hewitt, who five years earlier scored the winner against Real Madrid in the Cup Winners' Cup Final, and I conceded my first goal as a professional. I almost got it – at full stretch to my left, it evaded my fingertips, and Rony Francois later told me it was a beautiful dive. I recovered, made another save or two, and then was beaten by Hewitt again, this time from the penalty spot.

Before the final whistle I had a moment to look around, appreciate again where I was and what I was doing. Above the stadium the night sky was black, the stars washed out by the glare of the floodlights. To my right, the main stand, angling away from me, was filled with identical-looking rows of heads, bundled against a stinging ocean wind that swirled across the pitch. Just a few weeks prior, I'd been stealing sleep while on the clock for five dollars an hour. Now I was playing a team which had known European glory, who had been managed by Sir Alex Ferguson not that long before. I tried, and failed, to make it feel real.

At the final whistle I was slightly mystified, undeniably surprised that I'd suffered no catastrophes in two separate games. John Kerr Jr, injured in the Celtic game, approached me on the pitch in street clothes to tell me how well I had played. Several others were equally effusive, but not Winnie. He pointed out that I stayed on my line for a ball I should have come for, and came rushing out for one I should have left for my defenders. This was true, though I got away with both errors of judgment, which perhaps is what rankled him. To Winnie, dealing with crosses is the Holy Grail of goalkeeping, and there is no greater sin than staying on your line and forcing your defenders to handle what should be a goalkeeper's ball. He had been making this point since the previous summer, and it was reinforced to me from multiple sources while I was in England. I got it; but until I demonstrated it better in games, Winnie was going to keep on at me.

He couldn't have failed to notice that I had otherwise handled myself well, but if so, he kept it to himself. He wasn't interested in coddling or congratulating me, but educating me. There were times when I craved a pat on the back from him, but he didn't work that way. Better this, I told myself, than indifference. If he had simply ignored me, I would have been devastated.

I struggled to hide my delight at having twice played well, but I had to, because the fact was, we'd lost all three games we'd played. We weren't a real team playing real games, of course; we were a group of players from several different teams, brought together to play a series of friendlies. But nobody likes to lose. Once I got past my selfish pleasure at having played well, I too was disappointed that we hadn't been more competitive.

We had a night out in Glasgow, where Ajit and I ran into Mo Johnston and Kevin Drinkell of Rangers in a quiet pub. Kevin remembered playing against us the previous summer, when he was with Norwich. He said he would always remember the nightmare of playing in midday Orlando heat. Later, when we were all at The Cotton Club, a trendy spot at that time, I met a pretty girl and did my best to flirt. But the club was packed, I found myself gulping for deep breaths, and felt tremors of something that seemed like panic. I pushed it from my mind, tried to drown it in beer, but it persisted, a nagging tension. I stared wildly around the room, looking for exits. I finally slipped away when the girl went for another drink, and went back to Jordanhill alone. Even back on the dark, deserted campus, I couldn't shake the feeling, and only fell asleep after walking myself to exhaustion for hours around the grounds.

Whatever that episode was, I forgot it in the days that followed. We moved base from Glasgow to Fife, leaving Jordanhill College behind, in preparation for our final game, against Dunfermline Athletic. They were the only non-Premier Division team we would play, and therefore, with no small measure of naivety, we considered them our best chance for victory prior to the tour. Having lost the first three games, they were now, of course, our last and only chance for victory. Our intensity in training ratcheted up another notch. Unfortunately, the bed and breakfast we stayed at had no football pitches, so we were forced to play 'jumpers for goalposts' in a public park.

The night before the game, John Higgins gathered us in a cozy lounge at the bed and breakfast. He told us how well we had represented ourselves thus far, how we had done our country and league proud. But winning is what matters, he said. If we get back on the plane without having won a game, we will never be able to remember this trip as anything other than a disappointment.

He was a wonderful speaker, measured and deliberate and very sincere. I didn't know how the other players felt, but John made me feel like he genuinely cared about me, both as a player and a person. I was only on this trip because he moved heaven and earth to make it happen.

I was ready to run through walls for him. Then he announced the starting eleven: instead of Winnie in goal, it would be me. John had decided that I deserved a start.

It was exciting and flattering. The truth is that by the time I came on in the two previous games, the results had already been decided. I had played well, but with little at stake as far as the results. It's not the same as starting. This was going to be far more nerve-wracking. My stomach turned the moment John made the announcement, and I had difficulty sleeping. During the previous two weeks, I'd gone some distance in proving myself to the people in that room, but this game was going to be different. Everyone desperately wanted to win. We were suddenly like a team fighting relegation. John told us that Dunfermline was taking the game even more seriously than our previous opponents. They don't get to play a lot of international matches, friendlies or not. They would be starting many of their first team players, and a good crowd was expected.

The worst thing about the bed & breakfast? No table tennis. Nothing to do all day. I finished my book. We sat around, waiting for lunch. I took a walk alone afterward, afraid to go too far in case I got lost. The nerves steadily built. There is no pressure in football comparable to what a goalkeeper feels before a game. It is far easier to be the cause of a loss than a win. One moment of misjudgment, one mishandling, one failure of technique. This can happen to center backs or strikers too, of course, and be just as costly – but only in rare cases. I reminded myself that with nerves come greater focus, and adrenalin for more explosive energy, but it was empty. I held my right hand in front of my face and watched the fingers tremble so fast they were almost a blur. This could not be a good thing.

It was with both relief and dread that we finally piled into the bus and headed for Dunfermline's East End

Chapter 5

Park. From the moment we arrived, the feeling was different. Aberdeen, St. Mirren, and especially Celtic had treated us with polite but amused curiosity, verging on condescension. Dunfermline, by contrast, felt lawless. A few dozen fans mingling outside the ground jeered us aggressively as we walked in. I dressed quickly and rushed onto the pitch to start working the nerves out of my system. The gates were still closed, so the ground was empty, but they opened while I was still stretching in the goalmouth, and hundreds of fans – mostly teenagers and kids – literally sprinted into the terracing directly behind me. There were a few calls of "Alright mate?" and "Good luck, son," but mostly it was along the lines of "You're going to get fucking hammered!" A few kids started a chant directed at me: "Skinny! Skinny!" Once their numbers grew, they began leaning over the plywood advertising boards and beating on them with their fists. The din was incredible. Our players continued warming up, pretending as though we went through this all the time, but the effect was immediate and obvious: everyone was intimidated.

It was a cool night, but I sweated through my jersey before we retreated back to our dressing room. I put in a hard shift in the warmup, which forestalled the nerves, but only temporarily. I admitted to Ajit that I was bricking it, and showed him my trembling fingers as evidence. He laughed and admitted his own nerves. Oyvind caught my eye and walked across to me.

"Justin," he said, softly but firmly, "the boys really believe in you. You've played two good games. You can do it again. Come on!" He pounded my back and moved on to exhort someone else. A warm feeling spread through me. Oyvind had picked a very good time to finally display some confidence in me. Fuck these nerves, I thought. This is easy, this is nothing. That crowd is going to see how good I can be.

We when took the pitch, side-by-side with the Dunfermline players, I saw the terracing behind my goal was now completely full, as was most of the main stand. As I ran into goal, they jeered and waved, but it was a bit more good-natured now. I applauded them and they applauded right back, and then we were off.

The first twenty minutes felt like one extended car crash. We couldn't clear our lines, couldn't keep track of blistering, overlapping runs and mean, angled passes. In front of me, Ajit, Chopper, and Robert Heilmann were working miracles, lunging to tackle or block shots, but they kept coming in waves. We lost track of a player at the far post and he looped a header back across the face of goal. Great, I thought. It's going to drop in over my head. The crowd noise swelled and crested like waves crashing on a beach. But my feet, powered by the nerves and adrenalin, chopped at the grass and got me back to my line. I leapt and turned it over the bar with my right hand, before tumbling into the net. The crowd applauded. We cleared the corner, but a few minutes later came another header from almost the same spot, this one nodded firmly to my right, the near post. Again the crowd thought they'd scored. I twisted high, got both hands behind it, and held it. I couldn't help doing something silly then – I turned and showed the crowd the ball and laughed, then kicked it as far up the pitch as I could. The nerves, the crowd, the moment had turned me into one of the silly showman-type keepers I have always disdained. Perhaps I had been too quick to judge. Put me in front of a real crowd, and it turns out that I'm a ham.

Later, John Higgins told me that when he saw me do that, he knew it was going to be a good night. At that moment, though, we were still taking a battering.

Chapter 5

Eventually, though, we settled down and managed to keep possession a bit. When we finally strung a few passes together and started making some decent runs, we caused them problems. They were big and powerful but not particularly fast, especially in the middle, and Oyvind started to dictate play there. I remained busy, but it was manageable, just some mishit shots from distance. I could feel the end of the first half approaching, the end of my night's work, my Scotland tour, when we silenced the ground with a goal. Dunfermline made a hash of clearing a corner, and Sammy Okpodu, a Nigerian striker, pounced to finish. Perfect. Let the whistle blow, let me turn it over to Winnie with us one-nil up, job done.

Instead, the goal seemed to re-energize our hosts, and they came steaming right through the middle of the pitch. We blocked one shot, it rebounded to the top of the box, they hit another. It was a bullet but I had it covered, two steps to my left – until it struck a shoulder and spun viciously back to my right. I changed direction frantically, dove, stretched, managed to get a finger to it, but it wasn't enough.

The crowd behind me, teased and pent up for so long, erupted. Lying on my stomach, I refused to move or look up. You'll often see this reaction from keepers after conceding. It's a form of denial. I could just lie here forever, I thought. I let someone else fetch the ball from the net, we kicked off, and the ref immediately blew for halftime. I had been so close.

The disappointment of conceding was short-lived. There was nothing I could have done about the goal, and once again I had played well. My tour was over. No disasters, no calamities, no mistakes of any kind, really. Maybe a cross or two I might have come for, maybe a goal kick or two that might have been better (my hamstring had continued to bother me, hampering my kicking a bit), but on the whole, I'd justified John's faith in me, and had proven myself to the other players. Giddy euphoria replaced my nerves and made me hyperactive. I stayed on the pitch to help Winnie warm up, and the fans along the advertising boards who had heckled me during my warmup all smiled now – "Great performance, big man," and "Why don't you come play for us?" My chest swelled, but I played it cool, just nodded back with a half-smile – as if I did it all the time.

The second half was storming, chance after chance at each end. Dunfermline forged ahead with a well-taken goal in the 70th minute, after which we completely dominated, determined not to lose. The Dunfermline keeper – I'd been paying close attention to him, since he had the job I ultimately wanted – kept out a string of chances before we finally equalized right on full time. We would all have happily taken a draw, but it turned out that Dunfermline had billed this friendly as an international challenge match, and gone through the trouble of having a cup engraved. We therefore needed a winner. The tannoy said that if the match was still level at the final whistle, we would proceed directly to penalties.

Hearing that in the dugout, I turned immediately to John and said, "Put me in for the penalties." It was audacious – that was Winston DuBose out there, after all – but he considered it for a moment and slowly said, "Alright son. Let's run it by Winnie. He's the senior keeper."

At the final whistle, while the players shook hands, we approached Winnie, and John said, "What do you think about letting the boy have the penalties?" Winston said, "Sure, he can handle them, I'll take one, whatever you need." John turned to me and said, "They're all yours." I didn't have time to thank Winnie – I had to run back to the

Chapter 5

dressing room for my gloves. By the time I returned, both teams had already selected their shooters, and the Dunfermline keeper was waiting for me at the same goal I played in during the first half, in front of the packed terrace. I trotted down to join him, raised my hands to applaud the crowd, and they all responded in perfect coordination, a forest of upraised arms.

It's a great but accepted myth in football that penalties are "nerve-shredding" for keepers. This is preposterous. We're not expected to make saves. The pressure is all on the shooters. We can only play the hero, not the villain. The villain will be the poor soul who misses the critical penalty. Penalties are a chance to have everyone looking at you, all the attention without the pressure.

Dunfermline shot first. I took my place on the line and looked over to the touchline. John and all our players stood up in front of our dugout, shouting encouragement at me. I could feel the nervous energy wafting off them and realized how helpless they must have felt. Some shooters give away which direction they're going to shoot by the way they approach the ball, where they point their plant foot, or how they open or close their hips to the target. I didn't get any of these hints from the first shooter, but I did have a strong feeling that he was going to my left, and I took off that way just as he struck the ball. It was the perfect height, about three feet off the ground, struck with pace but not quite close enough to the corner. I got both hands to it and turned it around the post. A comfortable save, but the kind that looks spectacular. The crowd groaned, then politely applauded, as I bounced to my feet and shook my fists in celebration towards our dugout.

The nerves returned as we took our turn to shoot, but Oyvind calmly slotted his into the net. I faced down the second shooter, and it seemed he was staring a bit too obviously to my left, an old trick. He'd just seen me fly across my line that way and kept one out; no chance he was going that way too. Almost as if we had planned it in advance, I dove to my right just as he shot there, got both hands to it, and held it. Our shooters in the center circle and the rest of the team in front of the dugout went mad. I'd saved the first two penalties. I stood, feeling dazed. Things this good don't happen to me. I tossed the ball back to the ref with a giant, stupid grin on my face.

We scored again. Dunfermline, unbelievably, missed again, this time without my help. The shot was out of reach, but also too high. It smacked off the crossbar. Score again and it's over, but this time we missed, keeping Dunfermline alive. I was well-beaten by their fourth attempt, but the cheer from the crowd was muted. They knew it was all but over, and Sammy Okpodu made it official as he buried his shot. We won.

In between shots, I'd kept up a steady patter of dialogue with the Dunfermline keeper, who mostly just smiled indulgently at me in return. I shook his hand, it turned into a hug, and then my teammates jumped on me. I broke from them and applauded the crowd again, and this final time, they were not merely polite but genuinely enthusiastic. I heard cries of "Brilliantly played!" and "Well done, big man!"

So there I was, standing in front of a wall of supporters applauding me, my teammates congratulating me. Just turned twenty-three years old, my apprenticeship served, my lessons learned. At the start of a brilliant career full of moments like this, attention and achievement and even, in its small way, glory. It wasn't even a conscious thought, just a new state of mind: I'm a professional, I deserve this. It will always be like this.

6

The high lasted for days. As we prepared to fly back to Florida, I spontaneously decided to extend my stay. We flew together to London, where the rest of the Lions boarded a 747 for Orlando. I stayed. Dragging my heavy suitcase behind, I showed up unannounced at Broughinge Road in the evening, just as the Borehamwood players were finishing a training session. I didn't really know what I was doing there. Somehow, flying back to Florida, where only a handful of people cared about the game, felt wrong. I had cash in pocket and nothing pressing waiting for me back home, so why not?

I hung around Hertfordshire for a couple of weeks, accepting the hospitality of one of the Borehamwood players who offered me his couch. He was a police officer, and one night, took me in the backseat of his car on the job. It was terrifying. Every time he got a call, he flipped on his lights and rocketed down narrow, twisting streets with only inches to spare on either side. I was convinced a pedestrian would step into the street and we would splatter him. It was an exhilarating night, but I was glad when it ended.

Player turnover at Non-League clubs is common and rapid. Only about half of the Borehamwood players from the season before were still around. Tony Tilbrook was gone. I trained with them a few times, but was spoiled by stadiums and crowds, and had no interest in sticking around to try to win a spot. A cold rain doused me one afternoon, and I decided it was time to enjoy the Florida sun again.

Chapter 6

I came home feeling like the conquering hero, but of course nobody knew anything of my exploits except what I told them. I was out of contract, but I visited John Higgins in his office and he made it clear I was a big part of his plans going forward. The new ASL season was several months away, so the Lions put me to work doing coaching clinics, working with groups of kids a couple days a week. With this money and my savings from the Scotland tour, I was able to forestall a day job. I was back with my friends and could sleep late every day if I wanted, but I kept the drinking and late nights to a minimum. Though I was out of contract, I was thinking and acting like a pro.

I had just a few weeks to live this fantasy.

One afternoon I ran into a friend who said, "I heard John Higgins got fired."

I told him I didn't believe him, at the same time I knew it was true. Of course it was true.

It took several phone calls to confirm, and none of the players were ever given a reason. It was strange, because John's only responsibility to that point had been the Scotland Tour, which he not only handled superbly but also organized from the start. It had also resulted in the club's first trophy, sitting proudly in the reception area of the club offices. Within a few days, I received a letter from the Lions, informing me that a new coach had been hired, and that he and only he would be offering contracts to players following preseason training in March.

I'd ridden the wave of euphoria for a couple of months, since signing the contract for the Scotland tour, but I could feel it all coming apart. A new coach brings in new players; that's the way it works. On the local TV news the next day, the Lions unveiled the new coach: Terry Hendricks. He had enjoyed a long and distinguished career as a manager, but his most recent experience was in indoor soccer. Professional indoor soccer. I had never concealed my distaste for this absurd game, fun to play but ugly to watch, and now the man with my future in his hands was coming to me from professional indoor soccer. The omens mounted.

I could only put the bad feelings aside and intensify my training, going out every day with Keith Ames or my friend Sean Carswell, a young goalkeeper. I got a letter from Terry Hendricks, inviting me, as a "returning player" (not strictly true, as I didn't play the previous ASL season) to a month of preseason training, beginning mid-March. The Florida heat, until recently tempered by cold fronts, was beginning to amplify by the time we met, all the Lions' old boys plus some new faces Terry had invited. There were four goalkeepers, including me.

Greg Kenney, an American a year or two older than me, had bounced around U.S. leagues for a few years. He was a friend. We worked together at goalkeeper camps and clinics the previous summer, where we got in a little trouble for opting out of a few "mandatory" staff meetings in favor of quality pub time. He was lean like me but a little taller. Greg was an unconventional thinker, not a typical footballer. He once told me that he wanted to try wearing one huge, oversize glove, with which to gather crosses, and one small, tight glove, to then control and hold them. He was serious. He took his golf clubs everywhere he went. We were going to get along fine.

Rich Hanson was one of Terry Hendrick's special invites. He came straight from the indoor league, and he looked it. He punched everything and could not properly kick a football. But he was quick and aggressive. And loud. Very, very loud. I could tell right away that Terry loved him, thought he had "attitude". He wasn't very easy to talk to, the product of an intensity that favored involved debate over casual chat. He was by no means unfriendly, but neither Greg nor I could forge any sort of chemistry with him.

The third keeper was Lou Cioffi. A veteran of the NASL, where he had been a contemporary of Winston DuBose, he was ten years older than the rest of us, immensely confident and capable. He was going to be on this team. That left Greg, Rich, and me to fight it out for the second spot.

Early summer heat hit hard as we began training. I was confident, fit, and battle-hardened by my early struggles with the Lions, the cold and mud of Borehamwood, and the success in Scotland. My feet felt light and fast. In early sessions, I performed well but immediately there was something not right between Terry and me. He knew Rich from the indoor leagues, he had apparently crossed paths with Greg at some point, based on the way they talked, and he was the same age as Lou. They chatted and shared a laugh, but with me it seemed strained and forced on the part of both of us. I tried a couple of times. He had recently moved down to Orlando from somewhere in the Midwest, and I asked him if he had seen an alligator yet. "No," he said, "not yet." For whatever reason, I couldn't think of a follow-up to that, so we simply looked at each other for a few seconds, until I saw Greg and Lou starting to loosen up and jogged over to join them.

Another problem was that he considered me a "returning player." The 1988 ASL season had not gone well for the Lions, hence Mark Dillon's dismissal, and Terry stated several times that what the players did last year was not good enough. I, of course, did not play for the Lions in the 1988 season, but it seemed he included me in the group who did.

Once the sessions began in earnest, Terry, who had been a goalkeeper himself, took the four of us for special sessions on a hard, sun-baked pitch surrounded by Orlando freeways. It was old school stuff, diving from post to post, for ball after ball, testing stamina more than skill. I fared okay; I felt like I was going to die after every dive, my legs turning to jelly as the up-down repetitions burned the glycogen fuel from the muscle. But I handled it better than Rich, who was frankly not very fit, and Lou, who had not played professionally anywhere in 1988.

Greg, on the other hand, trumped us all. Despite an apparently laconic approach to his work, he was insanely fit, able to fling himself back and forth across his goal for ninety seconds, then get up laughing. It inspired me. I saw a chance to put some distance between Rich and me, and tried to match Greg's example. I fought through the pain and blinding sweat as Terry's drills got more and more torturous. His favorite was The Triangle. He set up three cones ten feet apart. Each side was a "goal" we had to protect, with balls being served in rapid-fire succession by the other three keepers awaiting their turn. We started easy, thirty seconds, then extended it to sixty, and finally, a nightmarish ninety. If ninety seconds doesn't sound like a long time, keep in mind it takes only two or three seconds to dive and scramble to your feet. So imagine doing that thirty or forty times without stopping, as fast as possible. Your lungs burn and a thick metallic taste comes into your mouth as your vision narrows. Focus on the ball. See it. Save it. Keep the feet moving. The worst is when someone flubs the service, forcing you to break momentum and wait a split second while they struggle to shoot. It's like starting over. You dive and dive and dive, Terry is yelling at you to work harder, the other keepers are shouting genuine encouragement, and in the back of your mind, you're thinking, "This has to be the last ball." But it's not. There goes the glycogen, there go the leg muscles. Stumble and stagger the rest of the way until, mercifully, it's over. Ninety seconds is a very long time.

We ran, too. Short, hard sprints on the grass, or long street runs around downtown Orlando lakes. I had always hated running, but I wasn't bad at it. I tried to stay in the middle of the pack. Greg was always near the front, Lou a little bit behind me, Rich miles back. He had a big, boxy physique, great for the shot-stopping demands of indoor soccer, not so good for running. The players whispered rumors about punishing runs to come up and down the stairs in the massive Citrus Bowl, but thankfully these never materialized.

After two weeks, the focus shifted from physical to technical work. We began playing small-sided games. Communication and presence are vital for a goalkeeper, especially on a small pitch. Lou showed his class in these situations, while Greg and I held our own. Rich, to me, was struggling. I could see the stain of the indoor game on him, the way he was frequently on his heels, the way he punched shots away instead of catching. But I also knew I was being hypercritical. Seen another way, he was loud, confident, and aggressive. He had good footwork and could make saves. As the days went by, I realized I was in the fight of my life. I had no Plan B. I get a contract with the Lions and am a real professional, or I don't and I'm not.

After two weeks of two-a-day training sessions, there was still nothing between the keepers. Lou had the three of us over to his house on an off day for burgers and Italian sausage on the grill. Rich was more relaxed and easier to talk to away from the pitch, and we had a nice afternoon. The next day, from nowhere, Greg dropped a bombshell: he'd been negotiating a contract with Boston all week, and had agreed to terms. It meant the fight was now down to Rich and me. My chances had improved, but I was sad to see Greg go. He knew how to keep the mood light. Without him around it wasn't as fun.

We finally got to play some games. On alternate days, we played three college teams: University of Central Florida, Rollins, and Stetson. Terry divided each game into thirty-minute segments and gave each keeper a segment. None of us had much to do in a dull game against UCF, but everything changed when we played Rollins. I claimed two crosses under pressure and generally communicated and organized well. Lou did the same. Rich, though, got beat by what looked like a stoppable shot from twenty five yards, then got in a terrible muddle with Lou Karbinier, caused by lack of communication, resulting in Lou prodding the ball into his own goal. On the bench, Lou raised his eyebrows at me. Rich put on a great show of anger and anguish. I allowed myself to hope.

At training the next day, as we set off on an easy jog around a lake, I realized Rich was not there. Lou, trotting alongside me, said, "I think he got the chop."

Is that really it? I've made it? I played it casual. "I feel bad for him," I started to say. Lou cut me off.

"Nope. Don't," he said. "Not when there's money involved. Just take care of yourself, don't worry about anyone else."

The rest of the session passed in a haze. It felt unreal. I had worked hard for this, laid awake at night hoping for it, and now it seemed to be happening. And yet, Terry still didn't speak directly to me, except to stop a counter-attacking exercise in the middle to complain about my distribution. The familiar unease began creeping in even before the session ended. Sure enough, Rich was back at training the next day, smiling as if nothing had happened.

I started the third game, against Stetson. My thirty minutes were nearly up when a ball got played over the top. It was in-between Robert Heilmann and me. I started to come for it, hesitated, came a few steps out of my box, then realized that the striker chasing it had given up and started to slow down. But the ball skipped at me at pace, and I was out of my box. I tried to back up with it and collapse on it in the box, but I mistimed it, handled it just on the wrong side of the line. The referee – the bastard! – spotted it somehow from thirty yards behind the play, and gave a free kick for handball.

We survived the free kick, but given my situation, it nonetheless felt like a glaring clanger, and I didn't have a chance to make up for it. My thirty minutes ended, Rich and Lou took their turns, and it was over. Terry, for almost the first time, spoke to me afterward.

"I'm giving everyone a few days off, in turns," he said. "Rich's was yesterday. We don't play again until next week. Take the rest of the week off, then call me Monday morning and I'll let you know the schedule."

That set my alarm bells ringing. The rest of the week? It was only Wednesday. My body was sore and I was sunburned and exhausted, so there was no doubt I could use the rest. But I didn't want to be at home on my sofa while Rich was diving around and yelling and laughing in front of Terry.

"Rich only took one day," I said. "How about I just take one day too?"

"That was because of the game today. Take the rest of the week, it will do you good."

He was right, it did. For one day. Then I began to fret. My imagination ran wild, swinging from miserable resignation to needy optimism. I struggled to fill the days, and checked my answering machine constantly. The weekend finally crawled by. On Monday morning I waited until a respectable time, 10:30, and phoned Terry. He seemed surprised by my call.

"You told me to call today," I reminded him.

"Oh, right."

He was silent for a moment, just a moment. But I knew.

"I don't see where you fit in with this team," he said.

On some level, I had known it was coming from the moment I saw him on TV being introduced as the new manager, heard him say changes were needed, learned he was coming from indoor soccer. Before that, even: from the moment I heard John Higgins had been dismissed. In that instant, I knew that what had happened in Scotland no longer meant anything. All that trust and goodwill between player and manager – gone.

I wanted to debate Terry, argue my case, remind him that while Rich was playing rebounds off the boards in places like Scranton, I was making saves on the grass pitches of Aberdeen and Dunfermline. I started to mumble something along those lines, but he cut me off, not harshly, and said, "You're mature enough to know how this works. I have tough decisions to make. This was a tough one." I thanked him and hung up.

I was temporarily protected from disappointment by a numb sense of shock, followed by denial, and finally anger. I also felt mortified. All my friends had been asking every day how the sessions were going and when I was going to be offered a contract. What would I say to them? What would I do for money?

Worse, I didn't even get to make a clean break. Along with a few other players who were present during preseason, but not offered contracts, Terry told me I was still welcome to train with the team and sit on the bench during games, albeit in street clothes. I should have probably passed, but my pride forced me to go to a few sessions and the season opener, where I watched Lou perform brilliantly. The Lions went on a road trip after that, but when they returned I stayed away.

It's what I imagine divorce must be like. I lay awake at night, staring at the ceiling, replaying everything I did over and over, torturing myself with questions nobody could answer: what could I have done better? How could he prefer an indoor keeper to me? I thought again and again about the ball I misjudged and handled outside the area. That must have given Terry his excuse; he must have loved it. I checked the Lions' results in the paper. Like a scorned lover, I hoped they would suffer too, yet I couldn't quite bring myself to hate them.

I gradually broke the news to my friends and family. They were sympathetic, of course, but the well-meaning platitudes they offered only deepened my depression. I felt bad about making them feel bad for me. There were other teams in the league, of course, and I should have followed up, made phone calls, used connections. But I had made the Lions an all-or-nothing proposition, and failure drained me of spirit and resolve. I had nothing left to give to anything. I was in tremendous pain that engulfed me but radiated from no specific part of my body. I resisted all attempts to ameliorate it.

Every minute of every day felt like a breaking point. There was an event horizon ahead of me, just out of sight, and I was rushing headlong into it.

7

Psychological and stress-related illnesses were not yet well-understood in 1989. Anything that manifested itself physically in the body must have had a physical root cause, or so the conventional wisdom went. That is why nobody could figure out what was wrong with me when I took ill: they were looking in the wrong place.

For a month after parting ways with the Lions, I alternated between cheerful denial and black-hearted, often drunken, depression. My friend Jeff, sensing I needed to get out of my own head, invited me on a Bahamas cruise. He worked for a cruise ship company, so the trip was free.

Together with a few other friends, we had gone on a cruise not long after I'd returned from the Scotland tour. It had been a blast. We snorkeled in the pellucid Bahamian waters, flirted with pretty girls, and pretended to be hardened gamblers in the casinos of Nassau. We laughed good-naturedly at the cheesy cruise ship conventions and orchestrated activities, most of which we ignored in favor of drinking from morning to night. I was happy and confident, and we had a hell of a time.

But when Jeff and I departed for our cruise, I was not happy. I was harboring a deep and abiding hurt, which I tried to mask for the sake of those around me. I didn't want their pity; pity meant I had failed. The energy I expended trying to act happy exhausted me. Despite this, I struggled to sleep, lying awake night after night, analyzing what had gone wrong in infinitesimal detail. I drank too much, too frequently, and ate poorly. By the time the cruise ship left port, I was little more than a lifeless husk with a fake smile.

Chapter 7

On our second day in the Bahamas, we landed at a small out island. Before lunch I was ravenously hungry, but after taking three bites of pasta, my stomach convulsed and I was overcome by nausea. I excused myself from the table and returned to our little cabin, where I laid on the bed with my knees pulled up to my chest until the nausea passed. Although it did, the same thing happened at dinner: a few bites of food, followed by a sudden, paralyzing wave of nausea. I spent the rest of the cruise afraid to eat.

Over the next few weeks, a feeling of vague, persistent nausea stayed with me. I assumed I'd picked up some kind of tropical bug that would run its course, but it only got worse, the episodes occurring more frequently and lasting longer. Finally, one night I was overpowered by it. It left me curled in a ball, clutching my stomach, awake until the sun rose. I could no longer pretend whatever was happening was going to go away on its own.

So began a months-long saga involving every possible medical exam: blood tests, barium x-rays, vision and hearing tests, even an endoscopy -- a camera down my throat and into my stomach. All tests were negative. The best a series of doctors could come up with was a generic diagnosis, gastritis, which was really just the term for my main symptom: an upset stomach.

My routine was the same almost every day: I awoke feeling well and ate a full breakfast. But breakfast never really seemed to settle or digest. Lunchtime came and went without me feeling hungry. Eventually my stomach would start to cramp a bit and my blood sugar dropped, so in late afternoon I would choke down half a sandwich and maybe a banana. Dinner, most nights, was often just a bowl of cereal.

I tried to make the most of breakfast, loading up on French toast with butter and powdered sugar for maximum calories, but it only served to further blunt my appetite during the rest of the day. I took in a thousand calories a day on a good day, far less on a bad one – and there were lots of bad ones. Acute nausea attacked me two or three times a week, almost always late at night. I walked alone through my sleeping neighborhood, taking small sips of Emetrol, an over-the-counter stomach medicine, until the attacks passed.

After a month of this, I was almost unrecognizable. Twenty pounds had vanished from what had already been a lean and rangy frame. I'd never had any body fat, so the lost weight was entirely muscle. You can't lose twenty pounds without people noticing. Friends were tactful, but the occasional acquaintance couldn't help blurting out, "What happened to you?" or "Are you okay?" I always said the same thing: I just got over the flu, it's just water weight, I'll put it right back on. But it only got worse. By midsummer, my normal weight of one-hundred and sixty pounds had withered down to one-hundred thirty two. More visits to doctors, more medicines. They tried Reglan, a drug designed to speed up the passage of food from the stomach, to no avail. Stomach acid blockers did no good. Carafate, designed to repair damage done by acid to the stomach lining, was equally ineffectual.

A psychological element soon manifested. I began to feel like an unwell person, as if there was something terminally wrong with me. All the deadly things had been ruled out – cancer, AIDS – but I couldn't help but feel the doctors had missed something, and it was eating me away from the inside. Food seemed to be the root of all my problems. I felt sick all the time, but especially after I ate. My body seemed to want to vomit, though it never did.

Chapter 7

Instead of becoming inured to the feeling of nausea and the idea of vomiting, I began to fear it, and the easiest way to prevent it was to simply not eat. I convinced myself that even at one-hundred thirty two pounds, I looked just fine. I ate less and less.

A beer or two might have relaxed me, and the calories would certainly have been welcomed, but ironically, when it finally could have done me some good, I shunned alcohol. It seemed like just another thing that could upset my stomach. My drinking friends were frustrated. They tried to take me out for a good time, but I just stood in the corner, my clothes billowing loosely around me like a rain poncho on a child, sipping a soda. Because the nausea often hit late at night, I became steadily more nervous as the clock ticked, to the point where I could no longer fall asleep until I saw the sky beginning to brighten. I was up all night, alone, watching bad TV, and slept away much of the day. The weight loss and vampire hours lent to my face a pallid, waxy texture. The father of a close friend laughed when he saw me for the first time in weeks. It was a laugh designed to mask the shock I could see in his face.

Work was impossible. I had taken a job in a soccer shop in Orlando, and while I liked it as far as jobs went, it meant a one-hour trip each way, in my car with no air conditioning, in the blistering Florida summer. Hungry but nauseated, my hands shaking from low blood sugar, I nearly passed out behind the wheel more than once. I finally took an extended leave of absence.

Football was entirely out of the question. I didn't go near a ball for almost two months. My scrawny frame embarrassed me, so I stayed away from people I knew. A short walk from my neighborhood was a lake with a public gazebo. I went there in the afternoons to read and watch small alligators sun themselves on the muddy bank, often passing entire days doing nothing but staring at them.

I thought of my condition as a persistent sickness, like a bad case of the flu. When two months became three, and then four, I started to consider the possibility that I might never recover. I became hyper-aware of my stomach at all times. I marveled at how the rest of the world carried on. I watched people in shopping malls and bookstores, going about their lives, apparently healthy. They weren't worried every minute about keeping down their last meal and stringing together more than a few hours of sleep. Wonder soon turned to resentment. Healthy people seemed, to me, to be rudely flaunting it.

I eventually gave up on going to doctors. I had seen specialists, from gastroenterologists to ear, nose, and throat, and even eye doctors. They all had theories, but never came to any conclusions, and certainly never found anything that made me feel better.

Some days were better than others. One afternoon, I managed to eat a decent lunch, felt a burst of energy, and went for a long bike ride in the sun. It was a revelation: feeling good simply meant having energy, and you can't have energy without food.

The fix wasn't as simple as merely recognizing the problem, however. I still felt queasy all the time, still battled acute attacks of nausea a couple of times a week, still feared vomiting to the degree that it turned me into a germaphobe. But I did make an effort to begin eating just a little bit better. After another successful bike ride, I decided it was time to try playing again. I phoned Keith Ames one afternoon, and he met me for a casual kickabout. I felt unsteady at first, but soon settled in. He thumped shots at me and they stuck in my gloves. Maybe this isn't going to be

Chapter 7

a life sentence, I thought. I'll eat better, get stronger, put back on all the missing weight. The time away will have done me good. I'll find a new team, itching to prove myself anew.

More players gathered at the pitch for a pickup game. Most of them knew me, or knew who I was, and one of them said, with genuine concern, "Man, what happened to you? Where did you get those toothpick arms?"

I asked Keith: "Do I look that bad?"

He shook his head. "Nah."

But he was lying, and I knew it.

8

The optimism that came with the early improvement was as fleeting as the improvement itself. I did my best to eat more, but managed to replace only three or four out of nearly thirty missing pounds. I still had to dress to hide myself, wearing oversized t-shirts and tracksuit bottoms even on hot days. Football was an almighty challenge. I was too worried about how skinny I looked to either concentrate on, or enjoy, playing. I wouldn't go near an actual game, just kickabouts with Keith. I began to wonder if there was anything to look forward to; I mulled returning to university to complete my degree, perhaps go into coaching, where my weight wouldn't matter.

Shortly after the Scotland Tour, I had written to St. Mirren, Aberdeen, and Dunfermline Athletic, asking for a trial. None responded, and I forgot about it, especially after falling ill. Then I got a letter from Dunfermline. Jim Leishman, the manager, told me that he remembered me well and was impressed with my play. He said that his players were all under contract for the new season, but that I was welcome to come over and train with them, as long as I understood that it would be at my own expense. I'm not sure why I thought this was a great offer, but I did. One of my first thoughts was that Scotland is cold, and in cold weather I would be able to wear layers that would hide my skinny body. It didn't sound at all crazy to me. I did not yet realize the magnitude of my psychological disorder.

I hadn't been working much, surviving largely thanks to the generosity of my family, who were of course terribly worried about my condition. I began doing more

Chapter 8

coaching, training kids for twenty dollars per session. I also started to train more seriously myself, pushing my spidery frame in sessions with Keith. When I felt physically capable, or more accurately when I convinced myself I was, I bought a ticket and flew to Glasgow.

9

Dunfermline Athletic in the autumn of 1989, when I arrived, was a happy football club. Newly promoted to the top flight of Scottish football, early-season results exceeded even the most optimistic expectations. Veteran striker Ross Jack banged in the goals, Hungarian import Istvan Kozma pulled strings in midfield, and goalkeeper Ian Westwater worked miracles.

Training sessions were noticeably free of tension. Players laughed, bantered, took the piss. Everyone was welcoming to me, especially the other goalkeepers. Westy was a big, strongly built man, with thinning hair and an easy smile. He was only three years older than me, but was an established first-team professional and had the cool, protective armor of confidence that comes with that. His number two was John Hillcoat, known as Hilly, three years my junior. John was nearly as skinny as I was. Whether he saw me as a threat or not, we became friends almost immediately. There was also a pair of youth team keepers, both sixteen. They didn't train with the senior pros, but sometimes the five of us had sessions together, with Westy the unofficial goalkeeper coach.

Though I got off to a good start at the club, and within a week felt at home, I was living a life of denial. I tried to ignore it, to fight through it, but it was inescapable: I was still sick.

Through the excitement of my first weeks at Dunfermline, the acute attacks persisted. I stayed with a friend I met on the Scotland Tour, a student at Jordanhill College who worked as one of our kit men while we trained

Chapter 9

there. I caught a lift to training every morning with Phil Bonnyman, a youth team coach. By the time we made the return one-hour drive, my stomach had often begun to feel like I had a squid living inside me, and the most I managed to eat those evenings was a small sandwich. After a few weeks, I joined many of the youth team players in a boarding house in Dunfermline, which eliminated the commute but did little else to make me feel better. I tried to eat small meals or drink bottles of Lucozade to keep my blood sugar and energy up, but the truth is I almost never felt well.

Training became my refuge. The competitive spirit, along with the physical joy of goalkeeping, flooded me with endorphins. The pitches were green and soft, and just like the previous year with the Tour, I'd traded Florida's heat and humidity - great for a day at the beach but not so good for football - for Scotland's bracing climate. Hilly and I had fun every day. We competed to see who could be more acrobatic, while Westy, more of a positional keeper, smiled indulgently at us. After training, we played snooker at Eagle Glen, the club's training facility, or in town at a snooker club on High Street. At night we converged at our lodgings and watched live football or goals videos until we fell asleep. It was football heaven, or would have been, if I hadn't been so sick and weak every day.

The lodgings were a laugh. We lived in a four-story house run by a single mother of two sons. There were other lodgers, but most of the rooms were taken by Dunfermline youth team players. Many of them came from Glasgow, and I was amazed to find they were homesick. Glasgow was less than an hour away. Without parental supervision, they reverted to a feral state. Unwilling to walk down two flights of stairs to the bathroom, they'd fill dozens of empty soda bottles with piss. Most of them were sixteen or seventeen. I felt like an old man around them.

As footballers, some of them were promising, while others would clearly need to look for a real job when they turned eighteen. I wondered about that. They'd left school for this; what will they do if they don't make it? I mentioned this to Hilly, and he named three of them who had a chance. The rest, he said, did not.

Hilly was humble and warm and not afraid, in our one-on-one chats, to admit his fears and insecurities. Goalkeeping is stressful at any level, but especially when it's your living. As the reserve team keeper, he had to prove he deserved his paycheck every day in training, since he wasn't proving it in the team on match days. And training wasn't always easy for him, or for me, because of Shuggie.

Hugh 'Shuggie' Burns was only a few months older than me. He had played fifty games for Rangers before the Graeme Souness revolution made them a major force, prior to spells at Hearts and Hamilton. At Dunfermline, he didn't feature in the first team, and maybe for that reason, he was a major annoyance to Hilly and me in training. Every team has one of these players, someone who thinks he knows something about goalkeeping. They're always telling you where you should be positioned and what you should be doing. We played a lot of small-sided games in training, and I always seemed to end up with Shuggie on my team. He shook his head in disgust when I was beaten, and berated me if I was slow or inaccurate with my distribution. He wasn't a bad player himself. He covered a lot of ground and got stuck into tackles. But he didn't offer much more than that, and in the middle of one of his tirades, I contemplated telling him he should worry less about me and more about his own career.

Chapter 9

He treated Hilly exactly the same way. We laughed over our Shuggie war stories while playing snooker. Interestingly, he never said a word to Ian Westwater. I suppose it helped that Westy was huge, but it was mainly that he was the first-team goalkeeper and was playing well. He was above Shuggie in the pecking order; Hilly and I were beneath him. That's the way it works in football dressing rooms.

My favorite of Hilly's Shuggie stories concerned a reserve team game up at Aberdeen. They'd gone up by rail, a long journey, and were in the process of playing out a drab nil-nil draw when, in the 90th minute, a deflected shot looped up and over Hilly. He backpedalled furiously and leapt, but couldn't get a touch. The ball smacked the crossbar and landed in the six-yard-box, where an Aberdeen player rammed it home. Hilly, lying on his back in cold mud, looked up to see Shuggie glaring down at him. For once, he didn't scream and shout; he just shook his head and muttered, "We came all this way for *nothing!*"

Hilly and I continued to have fun every day. When the first team played at home, we sat in the main stand in suits, enjoying the attention we got from the Dunfermline fans seated around us, and watched Westy continue to play well. He was not gifted with exceptional agility or fast feet, but he compensated for it with great positional sense, anticipation, and safe handling. We watched them beat Celtic 2-0 in front of a packed East End Park. Westy withstood a second-half barrage. He was equally heroic against Dundee United a few days later. Miraculously, Dunfermline claimed top spot, albeit briefly, in the Scottish Premier Division. Reality would eventually settle in, but it was already a tremendous return to the top flight.

One day at training, I casually mentioned to Westy how much I liked the tracksuits the first team players had.

He agreed that they were nice, and we got back to work. The next day, he handed me a bag. Inside was one of the club tracksuits, along with a brand-new pair of top-end Sondico gloves. I was flabbergasted, but he waved it off as nothing. It was typical Westy. He had a very different temperament to the hyperkinetic Winnie, but the way both conducted themselves as professionals set a great example.

Every day, I kept trying to lie to myself that everything was okay. But even as I developed friendships, the stress began to grow. The boys at the house started doing more things together, and they always seemed to revolve around food. I tried to find ways of making it look like I was eating more than I really was, pushing my food around the plate, pretending I was so distracted by conversation that I'd "forgotten" to eat. But in close comparison to a bunch of healthy teenagers who inhaled bags of chips and devoured boxes of Chinese takeaway, it was obvious that I wasn't really eating. It was obvious to me, at least. It's possible nobody else noticed or cared. But in my mind, everyone was watching me, judging me. The inner turmoil only churned my stomach further, which made it harder to eat. I was trapped. The only time I could eat a decent meal was when I snuck into town on my own. Knowing I had the freedom to walk away from a meal - if I felt like it - liberated me, and more often than not, I ate. But I couldn't always sneak away. I managed it only once or twice a week.

I spent a particularly sickly, sleepless night roaming the streets, listening to my Walkman. When I felt sick, I walked. It helped take my mind off things, but it also encouraged a gloomy introspection that began to manifest even when I was feeling well. The more my stomach bothered me, the more I brooded. The angry punk I listened to as recently as the Scotland Tour, emblematic of

Chapter 9

aggressive health, gave way to moody, indulgent pop
intended for faux-depressed teenagers. I felt victimized by
my stomach. It isolated me. I started walking alone at night,
even in absence of illness. This was repeating a pattern
established on the Scotland Tour -- I needed time alone –
but now I knew why: I didn't have to pretend to be well.

Back on the training pitch, I began letting the
opportunity slip away. Again repeating a pattern, this one
established at Brentford, I was too happy to simply be there.
I should have been working harder, fighting like my life
depended on it. The problem was that it didn't. Whatever
happened, I could always go back to Florida and make a
living through coaching clinics and private lessons. I didn't
think any of this consciously, but I must have known it, and
I let it hold me back.

I'm not sure to what degree Dunfermline were
monitoring me. Manager Jim Leishman rarely came to
training. He stayed in his office, working deals, pulling
strings. Iain Munro, a former Rangers player, ran the
sessions. He was cordial to me, and we had a connection
that was good for one three-minute chat: he had attended
Jordanhill, where we stayed on the Tour. Phil Bonnyman,
the reserve team manager, paid me a great deal more
attention. While it was mostly to yell at me, he also took
time to instruct and encourage.

Someone decided I should be given a chance to
play. A Dutch team came to East End Park for an
exhibition game, and we cobbled together a side from the
youth and reserve players. Phil managed and gave me the
first half. We played behind closed doors, so the stadium
was empty, but it was still a thrill: I was wearing the official
kit in a representative (if not competitive) game.

I was nervous but confident at kickoff, but it quickly became apparent that our Dutch visitors were badly overmatched. I had nothing to do apart from pick up a few stray long balls and roll them out to defenders in space. We ended up winning seven-nil. The next day, the local paper had a picture of both teams lined up in friendship after the game. I was grim-faced and withdrawn, standing at the far right edge of the frame, already wondering how skinny I was going to look in front of the entire city.

Not long after that, Jim Leishman came to training and asked me into an office. He said he knew that I could play, that I proved that last year on the Tour, but that without a UK work permit, he couldn't even give me a chance in the reserves – which he said he would have done. He said he could recommend me to other Scottish clubs, but that I'd have the same work permit problem anywhere else. He recommended trying to find a Junior (Non-League) club, and said in the meantime I was welcome to continue training with them as long as I liked.

It wasn't particularly deflating. I knew the work permit issue was going to be a problem. The only chance at a work permit would be if I had been capped by the national team, and I was nowhere on their radar. I didn't see any other clear choice but to continue at Dunfermline until I tired of it. I was happy, as happy as my stomach and anxieties would allow me to be. And there wasn't much to come home to.

I relaxed at training a bit, and began playing better. In a five-a-side training game, I pulled off a series of difficult saves, prompting striker Ross Jack to clap me on the back and say, "Great stuff, mate." Doug Rougvie, a grizzled veteran of Aberdeen's European campaigns under Sir Alex Ferguson, had the occasional kind word, and once, astoundingly, so did Shuggie. But I could feel the air

Chapter 9

escaping from my balloon. These guys had contracts, jobs. I was an interloper. When I was on trial, it didn't bother me. Being on trial is a normal part of a journeyman footballer's life. Hanging around as a charity case is not.

I decided to head back to Florida and then plan for another season at Borehamwood. It was more a stalling tactic than anything else. Maybe something better would come up before then, but if not, Borehamwood at least represented a chance to stay in the UK, where I wanted to make it, and play football of some level.

I walked alone around Dunfermline Abbey as a pale gold sunset stained the ancient stones and scattered light through the vast, surrounding park. I looped through town, down the High Street past the Carnegie Centre and then East End Park. Night fell. My brain raced and I struggled to quiet it. I turned and repeated the loop, again and again, until after midnight, and finally went home exhausted, certain I would sleep.

The next day after training, Hilly and I played one last game of snooker. Westy and Ross Jack wished me luck. I said goodbye to the youth players and their bottles of piss, and then I was off.

10

Back in the warm Florida winter, I accepted an invitation from Mark Dillon to play for a new team he had formed: the Central Florida Lightning. The ASL, the league I had fought so hard to be a part of with the Lions, and suffered so grievously with for my failure, had already gone belly-up. The Lions were still around, presumably mulling their next move, but Mark, always ambitious, wanted to eclipse them. He started with an exhibition game against the Albany Capitals, another ASL team, at a municipal stadium in Orlando. I had a few training sessions with the team, which included some Lions old heads like Ajit and the Mackey brothers. Then we played the Capitals.

All goalkeepers get a game like this now and again, when everything goes right and you feel unbeatable. It was funny, because Keith Ames drove me from Merritt Island to watch the game, and I spent the drive admitting to him that I felt nervous and unsure of myself.

All the time I spent training at Dunfermline included only forty five minutes of actual match time, so I feared being rusty. But right from the start, I had that strange sort of focus that reduces the game to simple lines and angles, easy to follow. There was a surprisingly good crowd in the small stadium, nearly three thousand. I hadn't played in front of a crowd since the Scotland Tour. It gave me a lift and helped ease my nerves. After fifteen minutes, I'd already made two spectacular saves. The first, a deflected cross that looped over me high to my right, seemed destined for the top corner. I scrambled and dived at full stretch, and just managed to claw it out from under the bar.

Chapter 10

It got a big cheer, and a glow came to my face that I hadn't felt in a long time. Then, minutes later, I dived to touch a free kick around my left-hand post. I took a few crosses under pressure too, and though I was beaten once by a firm downward header, I pulled off more saves in the second half. We won 2-1. Paul Mariner, the former England striker and manager of the Capitals, asked me if I'd ever been capped by the national team. I had to laugh. "I don't think they've ever heard of me."

"Then they're not doing their jobs," he said.

Nice moment.

That night of relative glamor was both the beginning and end of the good times with the Central Florida Lightning. It wasn't Mark's fault. We had a good team. It's just that the league we were forced to play in, the Florida State League, was made up of pub teams scattered hundreds of miles apart. We played not in stadiums but in public parks, alongside youth games, the touchlines crowded with screaming parents holding up signs that read "Go Josh #8 We Love You!" and "Kick 'Em Bobcats!" We spent every Sunday driving to games that nobody cared about. We had to drive our own cars and pay for our own gas. Returning one evening from Gainesville, I blew a tire, and had to drive two hundred miles home on a safety spare at thirty miles an hour. I couldn't buy a new tire because it was Sunday night and nothing was open. Plus I didn't have any money.

At least training under Mark was always good, and I started to feel like a competent goalkeeper. Ajit remarked on the difference between me now and when I first came to the Lions. I always had fast reflexes and agility, but now, I had a much greater ability to control my penalty area, even with my still-scrawny frame. I came for crosses with confidence, I read through balls better, and my kicking was finally professional standard. I began to see games as a chance to display my ability, rather than frightful opportunities for embarrassment. At long last, I started playing with attitude. I looked at opposition players and thought, have you ever played against Aberdeen or St Mirren? Have you had crowds applaud you? Have you been the only American in a team in England? I copied the body language of Neville Southall, my new favorite goalkeeper after Ray Clemence retired. I didn't have much of a chest, but I tried to puff mine out like he did. Here I am, it said. Come beat me if you can.

It didn't all go quite so smoothly, though. In the midst of all this good, confident goalkeeping, I made a howler of a mistake. Against some anonymous team in a game where I'd already made a few good saves, I came racing out of my box to clear away a ball, took my eye off it for a fraction of a second as a striker closed me down, and - *whiiiiiffffff* – completely missed it. It ran off toward the corner flag, I scrambled back to goal, but the striker, while falling off the pitch, miraculously hooked it into the empty net. Thankfully we went on to win the game, which meant my teammates saw the funny side, but Mark Dillon didn't. He reminded me that good goalkeeping is about managing the game, not just making saves. "What's the point of making saves if you're going to go and do something like that?" he asked.

I had an understudy, Quinn. He was a few years younger than I was, a promising goalkeeper who was eager to learn. His father came to our games, and as Quinn told me, "He says I should watch you and learn."

Now that's different. I'd watched and learned from Winnie and Westy. I hadn't been on the other side. There was temptation to play the big shot, and I talked with Quinn a lot and tried to help. But I couldn't let myself really enjoy it, because, of course, I compared myself to Winnie and Westy. I was starting to become confident in my ability as a goalkeeper, but I didn't have any real standing in the game. I'd never been a first-team professional goalkeeper like they had. So when Quinn and I discussed goalkeeping, I almost always referred to anecdotes about my own heroes, rather than offer myself as any kind of example.

Finally though, I got bored of my own insecurities. There was no epiphany; I was simply tired of feeling like I wasn't worthy of any attention or praise. The new attitude served me well in the remaining Florida State League games, but this only highlighted how meaningless the games were. I make a good save or claim a cross in traffic, but there's nobody watching. Spring turned hot. The pitches burned out under the sun and the six-yard boxes churned to dirt. I have a great, irrational hatred of dirt. Beach sand I love, but Florida's fine, insidious gray dirt is maddening. It cakes my gloves and ruins the grip, kicks into my eyes during goalmouth scrambles, hangs in suspension in the air. There are great pitches in Florida, but we didn't often get to play on them.

Bristling storms swept across the state from the west every afternoon, spitting lightning. We watched World Cup '90 games in the afternoons before training. The Lightning did well. We played our last game of the season, the league championship. It went to penalties and I saved the last one, so we won. We celebrated as youth games raged on the pitches surrounding us.

I made arrangements to return to Borehamwood. It was going to take money. I needed a plane ticket and a reasonable chunk of money to live on, in the entirely likely event I couldn't earn any in England. The good news was that the Wood now had a reserve side playing regular games, so there would be no more sitting in the stand watching whoever the first team goalkeeper might be. The more I thought about it, the more I was able to convince myself I was justified in continuing to chase the dream. I didn't pretend I wasn't still sick; by then, I'd begun to accept I always would be.

11

Shortly after returning to Borehamwood, to the same lodgings I had in 1988, on Red Road, I realized two important things: the first was that I was no longer driven to be a full-time professional footballer, and the second was that I wanted to write. The two were linked and related, but it is perhaps disingenuous to say that I "realized" these things. Instead, I came to understand them without really explicitly considering the ideas directly.

I played a match on my first full day back in England. The reserve team had reached a two-legged cup final, with the first leg at Broughinge Road. I didn't know what had happened to the previous goalkeeper, but Harry Meikle, a mid-thirties Scot who had been a player during my first spell at the club, was now the reserve team player-manager, and he must have sent him packing.

We had a brief tactical session in the morning before the three o'clock kickoff. The only player in the reserve team I knew was Paul Ferry, who as a teenager had made his debut on the same day I had made mine in 1988, against Leatherhead. Most of the reserve players were teens. At twenty-four, I was one of the senior players. Harry Meikle was the oldest, and he ran the show from the back. We played a flat back four, which left a lot of space between the line of defenders and me, and unfortunately, all of them were slow. I spent a lot of the game clearing away balls over the top. The opposition got onto the end of a few of them, and we ended up losing 3-2 to an injury time goal. I played reasonably well in spite of the goals, including somehow holding a full-blooded volley from no more than six yards.

Chapter 11

But I also developed some kind of mental block with goal kicks, and scuffed most of them along the ground. Something to work on, I thought. Just a glitch.

Through my first five games, it became a full-blown nightmare. Some kind of disconnect was at play, some kind of mental block, but whatever it was, I suddenly could not kick a football off the ground. During the return leg of the Cup Final, the fact that we overturned a 2-3 first leg deficit and won 3-0 was overshadowed for me by the fifteen goal kicks I shanked, sputtered, and dribbled along the deck. The small away crowd heckled me. I sent my half-volley clearances nearly to the other goalkeeper, but I just couldn't take a goal kick. During Florida State League games, I sometimes took goal kicks left footed, striking them well past midfield, for no other reason than I could. Suddenly it was gone.

I thought boots might be the problem, and overspent for a pair of replaceable-stud adidas. I hoped for a psychological boost, if nothing else, but it didn't work. My teammates and Harry Meikle were patient, likely because I was otherwise playing well. But obviously it couldn't continue like this forever. The root of the problem was that I was striking the ball above its equator and sending it rocketing along the pitch. When I tried to force myself to make contact lower on the ball, I overdid it and struck the ground, resulting in clods of mud and dirt flying farther than the ball. I avoided catastrophe somehow. The few times I struck it directly to opponents, they miscontrolled it, perhaps too surprised by their good fortune to take advantage.

The breakthrough came as I sat at home watching a game, envious of the massive distances both keepers were getting from their kicks. I watched closely... it was Everton versus Crystal Palace. Neville Southall did a funny little thing with his toe before he placed the ball on the six-yard-line. He prodded at the ground...he was making a tee! Why hadn't I noticed this before? I tried it in our next game, on a terrible, muddy pitch. The mud made it easy to form a little mound, upon which I perched the ball. Just seeing it up there, elevated a mere half-inch from the surrounding pitch, eased my stress. Instead of tensing up and trying to somehow force the ball into the air, I took an easy run and a smooth swing, and almost without feeling any contact, sent the ball soaring across the halfway line. It was the same with every goal kick, and from that point on, the crisis was over.

My interest in writing began on my first full day back, after playing the first leg of the Cup Final. Unable to sleep because of jet lag and the post-match adrenalin, I felt compelled to fill a sheet of paper with a detailed description of the game. At the top, I listed the date, opponent, ground, weather conditions, pitch conditions, kickoff time, and score. Under these details, I simply told the story of the game from my perspective. At the end, I awarded myself a score out of ten for my performance. I did it for the next game, and the next, and found I was enjoying it. I started to look forward to writing my game reports even during the games themselves. Something would happen, a near miss or a goal line clearance, and I would find myself thinking about how I would describe it later that night. Here's one entry, verbatim, from the day I sorted out my goal kicks:

5th Match: Saturday, Dec. 22 1990. 3pm vs Hoddesdon Town. Ground: Hoddesdon F.C. Weather: cold, overcast. Wind: brisk. Pitch: mud, mud, mud. Result: Borehamwood 0 Hoddesdon 0

Pitches literally don't come any worse. It was thick, wet, heavy, ankle-deep mud throughout. The penalty boxes were a disaster. It was so thick that it sort of sucked your feet down.

Chapter 11

I think this is the first time ever, at any level, I've put together three consecutive clean sheets. Once again, though, I was barely tested. I had a few through balls to come for, and I had two easy, unchallenged, near post crosses which I took comfortably at waist height. The only real shot was a low, weak effort from a free kick in the second half which gave me no trouble, even on that pitch.

The good news was my goal kicks. At last! I had about six or seven in the first half, and drove them beautifully, well past midfield. I did miss-hit two of them a little, but they were still decent. It felt so good, not having that total embarrassment of shanking them along the ground, which I had been doing regularly. Hopefully I'll continue it, and not miss-hit any more. My clearance kicking was good, too. I was using the firm ground on the outer edges of the box to drop kick, and I drove them nicely, even into the first-half wind. I had the wind at my back in the second half, but by then my boots were so mud-clogged that I wasn't able to really sail them, but I still hit them well. I didn't have a single goal kick to take in the second half.

I think my communication was a little better today, too. I tried to stay involved in the match, which was largely up at the other end. I did let my concentration drift a little in the second half, but I picked it up back towards the end.

Bradley had our only good chance, but the keeper was off his line well to block his shot. Naturally I was pleased to keep another clean sheet, and to have kicked well, but one of these days I'd like to make a few nice saves, just to show the boys that I can do it.

My rating: 7. Much-improved goal kicks (at last) and talking. Little to do once again, but I held it when it came my way.

Cumulative rating (5 matches): 6.40

I didn't consider myself a "writer" by any means, but I knew that I did have at least a passable facility for it. I had been a journalism major during my failed university experience at Radford, and though I was not widely or deeply read, I had always enjoyed books. My tastes were not eclectic. I read mostly horror thrillers from Stephen King and his imitators, or, when I was feeling serious, everything by Thomas Hardy. There were none of the standbys of the would-be burgeoning intellectual – no Hemingway, Fitzgerald, Kerouac, or Vonnegut – because I was not a would-be intellectual. I still thought of myself as a footballer, a goalkeeper. Most of my efforts and energies went into that.

When the first Gulf War began, I was as uninformed and jingoistic as everyone else in the Borehamwood dressing room. I didn't know the difference between a liberal and a conservative, I didn't care about saving the environment or equal rights for gays and lesbians. Footballers who pursued those sorts of interests did so at the risk of their professional lives. You get a reputation that way, as an outsider, a weirdo. Almost certainly, people would assume you were gay. In 1990, it was career suicide to merely be *thought* of as gay. There was a slippery slope of footballer logic that equated reading and intellectualism with homosexuality, so nobody at Borehamwood ever saw me with a book in my hand, but they all heard me commenting on the "tasty" barmaid. I'd like to say I was playing a part, but despite all the illness-induced introspection, back then it wasn't an act. That's what I was. Writing the post-match reports represented the first germ of growth.

The other influential factor was my gradual realization, after two years of steadily mounting evidence, that I might not make it as a professional footballer. It was true that I had been hampered by the lack of a work permit, and weight loss from my illness. But I was also short for a modern goalkeeper, barely six feet, and as good as I liked to think I was, it must be that I was not good enough. After

Chapter 11

five or six games for the reserves, I was enjoying myself and was glad I came back to Borehamwood, but I started to think ahead to a non football-centric life. I thought again about going back to university to finish my degree.

Even allowing myself to think this way eased some of the pressure I felt, and I enjoyed my football. It helped that the standard was not over my head. There were some decent young players in the reserve team, but no future professionals, from what I could see. Despite being an American and my usual loner self, I could tell some of them looked up to me. The youth team keeper, Graeme, said many times how he wished he had my athleticism, my "spring." I was more comfortable helping him than I was with Quinn, because I felt I was a little more deserving of being a mentor.

That's not to say everything went perfectly on the pitch. My back four was slow and, at Harry's insistence, held a line miles up the pitch, so I spent half of each game running from my box to clear away balls, and the other half dealing with forwards running through on goal. It was a suicidal way to play – if you have no pace at the back, you have to play deeper - but nobody seemed to notice it. I handled it all as well as could be expected. Except for once.

For a goalkeeper, sometimes there's nothing more difficult than a ball played over the top, coming directly at you. You have no angle on the ball so it's difficult to read. Is it mine? Does my defender have it? This happened to me at Broughinge Road on a dismal, gray day. Harry and my defenders were puffing after it, as was a lone striker, equally slow. It looked like the ball was going to bounce and roll well outside my box, too far away for me to deal with. By the time I realized I was wrong, it was too late. The striker collected the ball with his first touch just inside my box, took one more to settle as I belatedly came rushing out, and then finished with an awful, scuffed toe-poke that beat me because I'd mistimed my charge and was in No Man's Land, too close to him to react, not close enough to smother at his feet.

The ball trundled with agonizing deliberation into the net, almost seeming to pause on the goal line. Sprawled across the penalty spot like a soldier protecting his squad from a grenade, I let my forehead drop to the cold mud. I would have preferred to be anywhere else at that moment. Jury duty, root canal – anywhere.

Harry, only just catching up to the play, was incandescent with rage. He served an amazing volley of expletives at me. I clambered to my feet and nodded my acceptance. I had nothing else to do the rest of the game, no chance for redemption, and we lost by that goal. That's as bad as it gets for a goalkeeper.

I took refuge that night in writing. My match report was painful, because of the error, and left me unsatisfied. So I kept writing. I wrote about recent games I'd watched, and an Arsenal game I'd attended, mimicking the style of sports journalists I had read. It took hours, but felt like minutes. When I finished, I looked at the pages I'd filled, unsure what to do with them, unsure exactly why I did it.

With a dim awareness that this might be my last football experience in the UK, I strove to make the most of it, and caught two nice breaks. The first came when, inexplicably, Borehamwood FC were chosen to play the role of generic footballers in a TV commercial for Hi-Tec, a boot and sporting goods manufacturer. We had a rehearsal training day at the Douglas Eyre Sports Center in Walthamstow, where we played five-a-side on a lovely pitch. Afterward, Harry Meikle told me one of the people watching us was Alex Welsh, a highly respected goalkeeper coach who had worked with a number of top flight keepers. Harry quoted Alex as saying I "looked the part," and he said Alex had invited me back to the Sports Center to train with him, if I wanted to.

The commercial, filmed during a long day and night at Enfield F.C., paid much-needed cash, a hundred pounds, plus a pair of Hi-Tec boots and tracksuit. The boots fitted and felt great, and I loved the way the fold-down white tongue looked. My improved goal kicks got even better, and my half-volley clearances routinely dropped near the opposition penalty box.

After filming, I took Alex Welsh up on the offer, and once a week for the next five or so weeks, I traveled from Borehamwood to train with him. Tony Parks, the former Spurs keeper who won a UEFA Cup Winners' medal, was at a few of the sessions, along with Paul Heald of Orient (later Wimbledon). The sessions were amazing. I'd never worked with a goalkeeper coach like Alex, who combined a wealth of knowledge with a sense of humor and a natural motivational style. Goalkeeper coaching was in its infancy then, and Alex was at the forefront.

The pitches at the Douglas Eyre were lovely and soft, the late winter days perfect for hard work. We had fun, too. Alex had a drill called "Tales of the Unexpected" where he arranged large traffic cones around the six-yard box, then shot through them, the ball taking diabolical deflections at the last second. It was so much fun going through it that I didn't notice how exhausting it was until it was over. Alex treated me just like Tony and Paul and other, younger pros who joined the sessions from time to time. There was no doubt it did my game good. Alex preached far beyond the basics – footwork, positioning, posture. Having someone like Alex coaching me made me feel like a professional again, and it paid off in my games.

Off the pitch, though, life in Hertfordshire was testing. I constantly scrambled for cash. The Wood paid me twenty-five pounds a week, which was half of my weekly rent. I worked part-time behind the club bar a few nights a week for supplementary income, but the gig lasted only a few weeks. My boss was cantankerous and arbitrary. I missed a shift with a stomach virus, not debilitating but the kind of thing that doesn't let you wander far from a bathroom, and he acted like I'd personally wronged him. A week later, he told me – didn't ask – I had to work an unscheduled Wednesday night shift, a night I've been gifted a ticket to see a League game between Arsenal and Everton. I wasn't passing up a chance to watch Neville Southall and David Seaman in person, and told him I had plans. He told me not to bother showing up for my next scheduled shift. So, that was that.

The club sent a few more quid my way for odd jobs around Broughinge Road – painting a fence, picking weeds from the ancient terraces. Then, after the Hi-Tec commercial came my second big break: a Borehamwood fan asked me if I planned on attending the England-Cameroon friendly at Wembley. I laughed – the tickets started at thirty pounds. It turned out he was a television director at nearby Elstree Studios, and at his invitation, a few days later I was sitting on the set of *Minder*, a detective show, as an extra. The shoot took all day, much like the Hi-Tec commercial, but paid even better. With my frugal lifestyle, the cash lasted me several weeks. It was a lifesaver.

It was also an interesting experience, and somewhat analogous of my football career. The other extras were mostly aspiring actors. Some of them had enjoyed small roles here and there, but were forced to do extra work to pay the bills. It was tedious, frustrating work. They hoped to catch the attention of directors or casting agents, but when they did, it was almost always for the wrong reasons: overacting in the background or moving around too much. My director friend doted on me, coming over to check how I was doing every hour or so. The other extras tried to figure out what, if anything, made me special. I kept my head down and didn't talk to anyone.

Back on the pitch, our deathly slow back four began to take its toll. Although I felt as if I was playing well, I started leaking goals – twelve in five games at one stage. We continued to play suicidally high up the pitch, leaving me exposed at the back. One of our strikers actually gave voice to this at halftime of one game, saying, "Why are the other teams always running clean in on our goalie?"

But while Harry's lack of speed wasn't helping me on the pitch, his demanding demeanor was. Not that he wasn't sometimes terrifying, because he most certainly was. Except on rare occasions, he tended to completely lose his mind on us at halftime. I was usually exempt from these halftime verbal assaults, but on the pitch I was not so fortunate. Early on, he told me, "Justin, your handling and agility is top class, but you've got to do more to help your team." What he primarily meant by this was communication. He hated when I lapsed into silence during a game, but also disliked needless chatter. He wanted me tracking runs, alerting the back four to potential trouble. His other pet peeve was when I didn't make myself available for back passes. This was the last season goalkeepers would be allowed to handle back passes – we didn't know this yet, of course – and Harry wanted me coming to meet my defenders whenever they had the ball at their feet, so they could easily knock it back to me. The problem was that ninety percent of the time they simply hoofed a clearance without looking at me, and sometimes those clearances were miss-hit or went straight to an opponent, which left me scrambling back to my line. There were times when I expected a clearance and held my line, and then the defender suddenly turned to look for me, only to have the passing lane cut off by an attacker. This was when Harry went nuclear. I didn't like it, but it worked: I became more alert and aware of my other responsibilities beyond shot-stopping.

Off the pitch, Harry was a charming guy, and laughed off his predilection for outbursts. Recognizing that I would be spending Christmas an ocean away from my family, he invited me to spend it with his. We had a great time, sequestering ourselves away to watch videos of his beloved Glasgow Rangers. Harry was another influence, this time showing me what outfield players, especially defenders, want and appreciate from their goalkeeper.

Alex's coaching, Harry's hectoring, and the regular matches were all doing me good. I felt as if I was still improving. But at the same time, it was probably going to be all for nothing. At twenty-four, I was still in relative infancy for a goalkeeper, but I could feel the clock ticking on my career. It was not sustainable to keep playing for pennies. I started to think about my post-game journals nearly as much as I did the games themselves. Maybe it was time to get on with a sustainable life.

Openly considering this, and after suppressing the thought for at least a year, came as a relief. I started to understand that failing to make the grade in professional football was nothing to be ashamed of, that I'd done well and had great experiences in spite of handicaps, such as not having a British work permit and my debilitating stomach. It's great to chase the dream, but not such a bad idea to have a Plan B if it doesn't work out.

Chapter 11

The great thing about life in Borehamwood was the way I was thoroughly left alone. I was friendly with the other players, but we didn't do anything social apart from drinks immediately after games and training. They lived scattered around Hertfordshire and London. The only real friend I made unrelated to football was my neighbor, a young banker named Nick. He told me which pubs in Borehamwood to avoid – The Crown, apparently, was a great place to get tossed through a window – and warned me about the group of louts who hung out on the High Street, looking for someone to randomly slap. His work kept him busy, though, and I only saw him once or twice a week.

In addition to friends, a normal life would include some kind of interaction with women, but I had none. I wasn't very attracted to the English women I saw, nor them to me. In the style of the day, they dressed and cut their hair like teenage boys, and they smoked. During my walks in London, I looked shyly at Scandinavian and German tourist girls, but that was the extent of it.

I did, however, have one exciting bedroom encounter in Borehamwood. One afternoon, after training in the morning with Alex Welsh, I came home to an empty house. The midwinter sun vanished early as I succumbed to a nap. I awoke thirty minutes later to the sounds of glass shattering, and before I could regain my faculties, my bedroom door swung open. My instincts kicked in and I shouted something unintelligible. There was a shout - "There's someone upstairs!" then the sounds of two people bolting out of the house. I didn't even have time to be scared. I called the police and waited for them on the front step.

Less than a week later, we got hit again. I woke to muddy footprints across the living room carpet. The VCR was gone. The police remembered my name when they came back.

We lost two weeks to a rare blanket of snow. With no games or training, I continued to wander around London by day, and experiment with writing at night. It had not yet occurred to me to try my hand at fiction, a domain I still associated with intellectuals or academics. Instead, I watched games on TV, then wrote up match reports, like I imagined sports journalists did. Doing this put me in an almost euphoric state of energy. It wasn't long before I ventured away from football as subject. One night, as a distraction from my always lingering nausea, I began writing an account of the trip my brother and I made to visit our father in South Africa in 1982. At three in the morning, I was still writing, filling page after page in a notebook I had bought with loose change. My writing voice was uneven, an amalgamation of American and U.K. English, but I didn't over-think it. I just enjoyed it.

Football was no longer like that. I was relentlessly analytical about my own performances, and my feelings of self-worth were determined largely by how I had played in my most recent game, and by my cumulative rating average, which I knew to the third decimal point. The self-imposed pressure got to be too much. Spring didn't bring warmer temperatures, only more wind and rain. Florida's beaches started to look appealing again. I knew there was no football to go back to – still no real professional league, and the thought of another season in the Florida State League was depressing – but I was okay with it. I made a snap decision: I was finished pursuing football as a career, and was going to return to university as a writer.

I told Harry I was going home. He tried to convince me to see the season out, but knew that Non-League football – reserve level, no less – was not enough of an enticement. My teammates presented me with a small, engraved cup: "Presented to Justin Bryant by the players of Borehamwood F.C., 1990-91." I was surprised and touched, but no less ready to leave.

A final factor was that in addition to my ever-present stomach problems, I'd suffered a series of colds and sinus infections throughout the long winter. After an accidentally severe haircut, I was shocked by what greeted me in the mirror: sickly, pale skin stretched taut over the jagged bones of my face, dark rings under my eyes. Finally realizing that my scrawny body was not going to fill itself out, I had joined a gym shortly after returning to England, and dutifully trekked across town two or three times a week to work out. There was no magical transformation, but I did manage to regain a little bit of muscle tone and shape in my arms and legs. But bereft of sun, riddled by one cold after another, I looked like a victim of radiation poisoning. Florida's heat and sunshine may not be the best for football, but with football occupying less of my identity now, I started to imagine a healthier me, swimming in the ocean every day, getting a tan, and becoming strong under a sun that would cook away any lingering viruses and bleach the hair I would let grow long.

I played a final game, wrote a final match report. It wasn't sad but exciting. No more pregame nerves, no more fear of mistakes, no more near misses, disappointments, brushes with the big time. I might enjoy a kickabout with Keith again, but I was finished as a footballer. I would not play a proper game ever again.

Or for four years, as it turned out.

12

I woke from a fitful slumber, my head against a window, the dull hum and vibration of tires on the road filling the van. Other players slept around me, wedged into whatever spaces were available. Empty fast food containers and Gatorade bottles littered the floor. Outside, it was night. For a moment, I couldn't remember if we were on our way to a game or had already played. I-95, flat and empty, sped by my window. A few stars hung above the horizon. The dashboard clock glowed green: 11:37. We must have already played. Thank God.

At first, I had stuck to my plan to finish my degree. I returned to Radford University, enrolled in classes, and helped coach the goalkeepers on a voluntary basis. In an academic setting, my interest in writing blossomed into an obsession, neatly supplanting football. I read Kerouac and Hemingway and Celine, and was soon working on my first novel. A little journal called The Iconoclast published my first short story. As a student, I had the greatest of intentions, but despite my new intellectual aspirations, I still lacked discipline and motivation, and found lectures in topics other than literature to be a crushing bore. I passed a few classes, but I still had a long way to go, my progress was slow, and after sixteen months, I lost interest.

My father had lived in South Africa since the seventies. Now, big change was happening. Old enemies were talking, apartheid was ending. I remembered being in Dunfermline when the Berlin Wall fell, watching on TV and feeling like I was missing out. I saw an opportunity here, a chance to be in on history. I flew to South Africa and spent

Chapter 12

the next five months in Johannesburg with my dad. The revolution happened, but, frustratingly, I missed out again. There were demonstrations, rallies, happenings, but in a pre-social media era, I had no idea when or where anything was going down. I ended up watching it on the news, like everybody else around the world.

More rewarding was the time I spent alone in the bush, in the Kruger National Park and on the Wolhuter Walking Trail. I saw lions, elephants, and crocodiles, trekked after herds of wildebeest, and sat around campfires under a sky soaked with stars. I was young and it seemed as if everything I did, everything I saw, shimmered with romance.

I stayed up late every night and wrote. My novel hit 150 pages. It was terrible, but I felt as if I was learning. I didn't miss playing football at all.

But I had no friends and no job in South Africa, and couldn't stay there forever. I returned to the US after six months, unsure of where to live and what to do. I considered myself a writer, but nobody was going to pay me to sit around and write. So I took a coaching position at a small university in Charlotte, North Carolina, and, like a normal person, I met a girl and it got serious. I was there through the 1994 World Cup, and into the following year, when the girl and I both decided we wanted to live in Florida. We moved into a funky pad on a jungle estate in South Merritt Island, a one-bedroom apartment atop a detached two-car garage. An older couple owned the main house, and we had access to their pool and a dock extending into the Indian River. We watched sunsets, dolphins, and bristling summer thunderstorms rolling across the river from the west. Peacocks roamed the property. I took the perfect job, writing about football for a start-up magazine, and began a new novel, this one set in South

Africa and based not on what happened to me there, but what I wish had happened to me there. This one wasn't so terrible.

On weekends, we swam in the ocean or bobbed around the river in a little sailboat. My newfound interest in wilderness, stoked on safari in South Africa, found an outlet in the Merritt Island National Wildlife Refuge, a huge expanse of wetlands surrounding the Kennedy Space Center. It is home to bears, eagles, bobcats, otters, wild boars, and, especially, alligators. I bought a decent camera with a telephoto lens and spent as much time alone out there as I could get away with.

The only blight on this sybaritic life was my stomach, which continued to twist and cramp and grumble. But without the stress of regular games, without the worry about how I looked in my kit, it was more manageable than it had ever been.

There was still football now and then: a kickaround with Keith Ames, or a pickup game with other old friends. But I played neither regularly nor with any real enthusiasm. I much preferred being in the refuge with my camera or at the beach with my girlfriend. The Orlando Lions were still around, playing in yet another new league, the complicated-sounding United Systems of Interregional Soccer Leagues, or USISL. Lots of the guys I had played with were still playing for them, or for a team even closer, the Cocoa Expos. Keith had played for the Expos the previous summer, and told me stories of how the players had never been paid on time, or indeed at all, in some cases. Yet he signed to play again in 1995, and began nagging me to join him. I laughed the first time he suggested it, but to my surprise, began finding myself tempted each subsequent time he brought it up. $50 a game for twenty games, he said, just to sit on the bench as the number two goalkeeper.

Chapter 12

That's two thousand dollars for nothing. Two thousand dollars was a lot of money back then, especially to me. It still is.

Adding to the temptation was Ricky Hill. A former midfielder with Luton who won a few England caps, he was going to be the Expos' player-coach. Keith introduced us one afternoon, and I was instantly taken with Ricky's affable manner and utter lack of self-importance. Within a week, I was running around in the heat, preparing for the season. I signed my contract for $50 a game. I assumed I would be number two to the incumbent, Didier Menard, an athletic and capable young keeper. Two grand to sit and watch games for a summer didn't sound bad. I had misgivings, but I told myself I was being nervous about nothing.

It was for the best that I didn't play, at least at first. My reflexes, handling, and kicking had not suffered from the layoff, but my positioning and reading of the game had. There were times during training when I wandered badly out of position, or watched a cross drop right into my six-yard-box, having been certain it was much further out. I was also slow to react to changes in the direction of play, and without Harry Meikle in my ear, my communication suffered.

Countering all this was the fact that I didn't really care. I wasn't trying to "make it" as a pro anymore, so my stress level was way down, if not nonexistent. Like Shuggie Burns at Dunfermline, the Expos had their own resident goalkeeping "expert" who liked to yell at me whenever I made a decision he disagreed with, or if I failed to distribute to him, but now I saw it for what it was – a footballer who thought he knew something about goalkeeping – and just laughed it off.

Didier and I got along well, the pitches at the Expo Center were green and manicured, and training under Ricky Hill was inspiring. He was thirty-six, strongly built and still fit, although he said he preferred to be a player-coach who didn't do much playing. The sessions were short and lively, lots of restricted-touch activities and small-sided games. As the season approached, I found I was occasionally enjoying myself.

It was clear from our preseason games that we had a strong team. We played a 3-5-2, progressive for 1995, with Keith at right back, Dave Mackey from the old Lions days at left back, and Welshman Dylan Lewis in the middle, with a holding midfielder, usually Ian Gill (another Lions old boy) in front of him. Didier started the preseason games and I finished them, usually going in for the last fifteen minutes, after we were two or three-nil up. I rarely had anything to do but still felt rusty, though I played with the calm nonchalance of someone who wasn't too concerned with how he did. It seemed to work.

Regrettably, if predictably, the USISL had decided, in the grand tradition of American leagues, to experiment with the fundamental laws of the game. Instead of playing for ninety minutes, we played for only sixty, but with the referee stopping his watch every time the ball went out of play. It seemed pointless to me – the games ended up taking roughly the same time as a ninety-minute game – but that was just the beginning. Instead of throw-ins, attacking teams were awarded a "kick in," essentially a direct free kick, whenever the defending team put the ball out of play within thirty-five yards of their goal. There was no offside for this kick, which meant both teams crowded the front of goal as the ball was played in. It worried me. Having not played competitively for four years, my biggest concern, should I have to play in an actual league game, was dealing with crosses.

The strangest alteration was the accumulated foul law: if a team committed seven fouls in a given half, the opposition were awarded a modified penalty kick. One player was given five seconds to dribble in from thirty-five yards and shoot. This was borrowed from the old NASL, when it was used to settle draws, much like a penalty shootout. I was intrigued by this law. It was patently ridiculous, of course, but it could be fun.

The absurdity of tinkering with the laws glossed over a more ominous aspect of life with the Cocoa Expos: management. Ricky Hill was running the team day-to-day as player/coach, but he was not actually the manager. That honor was held by Rick Sandt, a successful local businessman who had been a big part of the soccer scene in Brevard County for decades. Keith, Dylan, and several of the other Expos had played for him at Florida Tech University, where he had used his money and overseas contacts to build a powerful program. It was difficult to know what, if anything, he actually knew about the game. He was no tactician, but he knew the difference between a good player and a mediocre one, and didn't tolerate the latter. We had crossed paths many times over the years, but we'd never actually spoken, and, amazingly, this continued well into the season.

Sandt's right-hand man was Colin Thomas, with whom I had a more personal, if not entirely untroubled, relationship. The summer prior to going to Dunfermline, Colin had recruited me to play at Florida Tech. I was flattered by the offer, but had bigger things in mind at the time, so after a few phone calls, I turned it down. It may not have been quite that honorable; I may have simply never called him back. I remember being both impressed and put

off by how insistent and persuasive he was. It was difficult
to know if he held a grudge or not, as his manner was firm
at the best of times, so I trod lightly around him.

We began league play by comfortably winning our
first four games. The substitution laws were very relaxed, so
in each game, once we had the result in hand, I went on for
the last dozen or so minutes. I didn't have much to do in
these little cameos, though I did claim a cross in heavy
traffic during one of them, which almost made me believe I
could still play. Didier was playing generally well and his
place wasn't under threat, until he dropped a bombshell: he
was going to Norway for a trial with a pro club there. Didier
told me Sandt and Colin had tried to guilt-trip him into
staying, but he was still only twenty-four, had his career
ahead of him, and wasn't going to pass up a real
opportunity like that just to play for $50 a game.

And about that $50... We each got a check after the
first game, but after the second, the third, the fourth...
nothing. It was not a good sign. The players traveling from
Orlando for training were supposed to be getting gas
money, too, but they weren't. My alarm bells rang, but the
new situation with Didier took precedent. If he went, would
I be the new goalkeeper? And did I want that?

We played the Orlando Lions, or at least the sad
remnant of them, in Orlando. There were a few names from
the past, but we'd poached most of their best players
already. In the parking lot I said hello to two of them, Mike
and Sheldon, and they pulled me aside for a private word.
"Come play for us," was the message. Their team was
struggling and they didn't have a reliable goalkeeper. I was
flattered by their interest and genuinely considered it, telling
them we'd speak again after the game.

Chapter 12

I shook hands with them and turned away to find Colin standing right in front of me. "Can we talk?" he said. I was sure he had heard me talking about playing for the Lions, but instead he said, "I know you were told you would receive $50 for each game, but we're only going to be able to pay the starters."

I wasn't sure how to respond to this. Should I remind him that his starting goalkeeper was about to get on a plane to Norway? Or that two Lions' players had just asked me to jump ship and join them? Before I decided, he went on.

"As you know, there's some uncertainty with Didier. I want you to know that we're going to be bringing in some top goalkeepers. You'll be given a chance too, but we're trying to win a championship here, so it's only fair we bring in the best players we can get."

I agreed that was fair enough, then took my place on the bench to watch what became a farce of a match. The Lions weren't just bad, they were abysmal. Most of them were just average college players home for summer. We were five-nil up at halftime without breaking a sweat. I played the last fifteen minutes, during which I conceded a goal to the only shot I faced, and we won 8-1. Afterward, Mike and Sheldon approached me again, and Mike said, "Forget about it, you don't want to play for us. I don't want to play for us either."

Didier flew to Norway. The top "new goalkeepers" showed up to the next training session, as Colin promised. I had to stifle a laugh; they were awful. Even the Lions' backup keeper, who had played calamitously in the second half of our game, was there. The other players didn't know what to make of it. Keith was certain I would play. I had my doubts.

As Sandt's right-hand man, Colin had a right-hand man of his own, Pat Dicks, son of former Bristol City manager Alan. I'd known Pat since he and Ian Gill played together at Cocoa Beach High School, and he'd always been honest about what was going on behind the scenes at the Expo Center. He approached me after training on Tuesday – we played Tampa at home Friday night – and told me I would be playing. When I appeared unconvinced, he said, "Who are they going to get? No. You'll play."

Ricky Hill didn't have anything to say about the situation, likely because he didn't have the final word. Two new hopeless keepers attended training on Thursday. Finally, after the session ended and Ricky spent some time on his cell phone, he told me I'd be playing.

My gut rippled with excitement and dread, a feeling I hadn't had in years. Nothing about it was pleasant. This had not been part of the plan. I was supposed to get paid to not play; now here I was, playing and not getting paid. I glared at Keith before I left for home. Your fault, Keith.

The nerves built through the Friday at work. At times I was busy and forgot about the game, but every time I remembered, my stomach lurched. Lunch came and went without me being able to eat. I tried to choke down a turkey sandwich later in the afternoon, and an energy bar on my way to the Expo Center, but could manage only a few bites of each. At seven in the evening, it was still sunny and hot, the air dead. In the dressing room, I made a show of appearing relaxed, laughing and joking around. Some of the players, guys I'd never really played with, snuck glances at me, probably wondering how I'd do, whether I'd be a liability. I reminded myself of previous challenges I'd risen to: my unexpected debut for Borehamwood, the Scotland Tour. Surely I could handle a USISL game against the Tampa Bay Cyclones?

Chapter 12

Warmup gave me a chance to break a sweat, burn some nervous energy, get my body moving, but nothing shook my nerves. There was a war in my mind between the nerves, promising doom and dread, and my sense of denial, the one that kept saying, "Kickoff is a long way off, we still have the warmup." And when that ended, "We still have to go back to the dressing room and change into our full kit." And then, "We still have to go back to the pitch, long way to go." And finally, "There's still the team introductions and the national anthem to get through."

But eventually the game began, and I was all alone in goal with my nerves.

I had a vision of me in the Merritt Island National Wildlife Refuge with my camera, or behind my computer, working on my novel. That's where I belonged now – as, surely, everybody was about to find out.

Yet I got the best start I could have hoped for. After ten minutes, Tampa's left winger brought down a waist-high ball and lashed it on the half-volley high to my left. I didn't have time to think, only react, and flung myself up and backwards, turning the ball over the bar with my left hand. I got a nice cheer from the small but intimate crowd, sitting on top of the pitch down my right touchline in a temporary stand. The corner came over at a nice height and I took it at full stretch, then threw it out to Keith to start a counter. My nerves settled. I was in the game.

I dealt with a few more routine shots, and late on made a save that I was very pleased with, turning a flashing low shot around the post with my right hand. By then we were 3-1 up – there was nothing I could do about the goal, a free header at the far post – and it ended that way. I pretended to be nonchalant, signed some autographs, mingled with fans and friends at a reception afterward. I was pleased to have played well, naturally, but more than anything was relieved I hadn't made an idiot of myself.

I didn't have long to enjoy it. We played the same team again the very next night, this time in Tampa. We trekked all the way across the state in a couple of vans, and again I was unable to eat before the game. The nerves built a little less intensely this time. I'd proved to myself that I could still play, and, crucially, to both my team and Tampa as well. That was half the battle won.

The Cyclones played at a lovely little stadium at the University of Tampa. We had a beautiful sunset, all reds and golds in the sky, and before kickoff I spotted Perry Van der Beck, a former Rowdie from my youth, in the stands. I wondered if Winnie was there, too. I didn't have long to consider it; Tampa swarmed at us right from the kickoff. It was a different game entirely from the previous night. Shots flashed just wide or over my crossbar. I made a good save with my right foot to keep out a close-range shot. The crowd – there was a good little turnout, maybe a thousand – went "ooooohh!" as the ball ricocheted to safety. I felt good, strong, confident. I had a sneaky feeling I wouldn't be beaten.

We survived the early onslaught, and by the second half, had the game on even terms. A looping header nearly beat me, but I got a finger to it and pushed it off the crossbar. At the other end, with just ten minutes remaining, we snuck a goal and silenced the crowd. In the dying moments, a Tampa player found space at the top of the box and shot low and hard to my right. It took my best to keep it out, but it went right to another Tampa player following up. I scrambled to my feet and dove to my right to cover the angle, and miraculously, he fired it directly into my chest, where it stuck. The crowd groaned in frustration. We won 1-0.

Chapter 12

Many scenarios had gone through my mind before Friday's game, but somehow, playing well twice and conceding just one goal had not been among them. What I slowly came to understand, through the coming games and training sessions, is that without being aware of it, I had developed a core confidence that was not subject to the whims and vagaries of momentary events. I had finally outgrown some of my youthful insecurities. If I misplayed a cross in training, I didn't suddenly become a bag of nerves, worried about what everyone thought of me. I knew I could take a cross, just as I knew it was normal to misplay one now and again. I still had nerves before games, sometimes intensely so, but I calmed down once the whistle blew. I played dispassionately, plotting my way through games, keeping to my angles, playing the percentages. The kick-in law turned out to be a lot of fun. Crosses separate the boys from the men, and I took pride in coming for and claiming as many as I could. I kept playing well and we kept winning, though the two were not always related: we won quite a few games five or six-nil. On such nights, we could have played and won without a goalkeeper.

Halfway through the season, Didier returned. He had done well in Norway, but ultimately not quite well enough to earn a contract. We were glad to have him back, but Ricky told me he was happy with the job I was doing and wanted me to continue in goal. The problem is that it wasn't his choice. Didier had performed well the previous season and Sandt trusted him. I, evidently, had not done enough yet to earn that same trust.

Ricky argued on my behalf and struck a compromise: I would play the first half of games, and Didier the second. It was the best Ricky could do, but it was the perfectly wrong solution: it satisfied neither Didier nor me, leaving us both frustrated and the rest of the team confused. A team needs to know who their number one goalkeeper is.

I was surprised by how much it annoyed me to share games. I was still deeply ambivalent about playing, but if I was going to play, I didn't want to play only one half of each game. A half comes and goes almost before you know it. Sometimes, my pregame warmup lasted longer. I didn't need to play football anymore. But it turned out that I still cared, still wanted to play well, and, especially, still liked the attention that came with it. Sitting on the bench for the second half of games felt like it compromised that.

Florida Today, the local paper, ran a big story with pictures about Keith Ames and me, the "local products" made good. The coach of a youth team asked if I would stop by his team's practice to say hi. "It would make the kids' day," he said, so I did, but it really made mine. A father and son recognized me as I was browsing a bookstore with my girlfriend. My old ego monster began to stir from its slumber. It was enough to keep me interested in playing, which was good, because the fissures in the Expos façade began to widen.

Apart from that $50 check after the first game, we still had not been paid. The players raised the issue once or twice, but Colin always said the money was on the way, and nobody questioned it further. Amongst ourselves, it was a hot topic. Those who played last season told stories of how it started this way – the paychecks simply stopping with no explanations or apologies. I had heard these stories, had raised them with Keith, but he had felt confident it wouldn't be repeated this season.

It got worse. The USISL had a rule that stipulated a minimum number of American citizens must be in the matchday squad. With a heavily British side, we often had to leave a player or two out. Usually it was Fidgi Haig, a Haitian striker who was brilliant in his prime, but who had suffered a series of debilitating knee injuries. He was surprised, then, when Colin announced he was in the squad to play in Miami on a Saturday afternoon. Colin and Sandt rarely traveled to away games, leaving it to Ricky, so it was he who did the math and realized that Fidgi could not, in fact, dress for the game. It was a long, wasted day for Fidgi, who didn't complain, but it angered the rest of us. It was understandable that money was tight, but there was no excuse for that kind of lazy mismanagement.

We had to travel to places such as Nashville, Baltimore, Richmond, and Greensboro on a tiny budget, eating at fast food joints, driving all night to avoid hotel stays. More and more, the players whispered about the money. Some had fulltime jobs, but others were getting by on part time or less, and counted on the extra income. The negativity brought down morale, even though we were winning. I began to enjoy the football less, though I was still playing well. It may have been that the novelty had simply worn off, that after four years without playing, it was always going to feel new and fun again at first, but then I'd remember why I had stopped playing in the first place. But I think it was the missing money.

Whatever the reason, it began to feel like a chore. With Didier eager to play, I considered simply stepping aside. For one night at least, I did just that. I concocted a ridiculous lie to get out of a home game for no other reason than I didn't feel like playing. A whisper of professional conscience somewhere inside me knew that this was wrong, knew what Winnie or Westy would have had to say about it, but I didn't have much difficulty ignoring it. When I returned to training, I was greeted by what was suddenly bad news: Didier was gone. He got another opportunity overseas and jumped at it. Colin and Sandt were angry, I was told, but this time they didn't panic. They knew I could play.

That meant no more skipping games, no stepping aside for Didier. But as the only senior goalkeeper, the cards were now firmly in my hand. I decided to flex this muscle. As much as I respected Ricky, I'd never thought there was a compelling reason for goalkeepers to do distance running for fitness. Put me through my paces in goal, make me do the triangle, sure. But long distance running was not merely a waste of time; for someone like me, desperately trying to keep my weedy frame from withering away to nothing in the Florida heat, it was downright counterproductive. So the next time Ricky started lining up cones for a fitness run, I casually ambled over to Pat Dicks and chatted with him as the rest of the side grunted and sweated through their run. Ricky knew the score. If he told me to run, I would run, and he knew it. But he also knew I was now his only goalkeeper, and I was not entirely happy. He never said a word or even looked my way, and I never again took part in a fitness run.

Again, there was a nag from my conscience, but I excused myself because I was playing well. As my ratings from my Borehamwood journal demonstrated, I could be a harsh judge of my own performances, but game after game went by without a mistake. My feet felt light as ocean foam, I was handling the ball cleanly, claiming crosses, cutting off angles, anticipating play, all with a battle-hardened confidence that was real, not veneer. After some games, I almost laughed in wonder at how fragile I had been during my early days with the Lions, back when the game seemed impossible and I was desperate to impress. In the first minute of a game in some football wilderness like Nashville, I casually caught a vicious volley struck right at me from six

Chapter 12

yards. The opponent looked at me quizzically, unsure if what I'd done was difficult or not. That's the way I liked it.

The problem – and it was a serious one – came when the novelty of playing again finally did wear off. The routine, for a couple of months - a pleasantly nostalgic reminder of younger days - began to feel like an intrusion. I was still struggling with my stomach, and the demands of playing were only making it worse. I forced myself to eat late at night in order to preserve my weight, and my poor digestion caused frequent sleepless nights. When this happened, I'd walk up and down the dock, watching heat lightning flashing high up in the anvils of thunderstorms somewhere over Orlando. The occasional moments of ego-boosting recognition and praise were not worth this. There were only a few weeks left in the season, six or seven games and then the playoffs, but the way I felt made it difficult to see it objectively. It seemed an eternity. I wanted it to be over.

At this point, by my count, I was owed $550. It was the money, yes, but mostly it was the principle. I was playing largely against my will, fulfilling a commitment. To hold up my end of the bargain but not be paid the money I was owed was a double insult. I was determined not to be a victim. After a desultory training session, I lingered, waiting for a chance to speak to Ricky alone, but he was in a hurry and my chance didn't come. I went home, called him, and explained that I was quitting. I was honest with him – I told him that I'd lost any interest in playing, that I was disillusioned by the non-payment, and that I was physically suffering. Ricky understood, but he was, naturally, not thrilled by the news. I was his only goalkeeper and had been playing well. Based on the panicky and frankly hilarious attempts to recruit a new goalkeeper earlier in the season, when Didier first went abroad on his trial, I was not going to be easy to replace. But Ricky had been around long enough to know when he was dealing with someone who had lost the heart to play. He had doubtless seen it before.

Colin was another matter. He called me an hour later. "I just had a very disturbing call from Ricky," he said. I repeated my litany of concerns to him, acknowledging but downplaying the non-payment and stressing the health factors, but Colin was stubborn and persuasive. We had a weekend, two-game trip to Chattanooga coming up. He convinced me to make the trip and play the two games, giving him time to find a new keeper, and he promised to pay me whatever I was owed as soon as we returned. It felt like a defeat, but I agreed.

When I met the squad at the Expo Center to head to the airport, my chagrin turned to anger when I realized Colin had already managed to sign another goalkeeper, a promising player not long out of university named Phil. What need was there for me to go on the trip if Phil was signed? In addition to my stomach problems, I'd also struggled with mild claustrophobia most of my adult life. It seemed to come and go, but was exacerbated by stress, and that summer it made flying an ordeal. The last thing I wanted to do, the very last thing, was get on a plane to fly to Chattanooga to play whoever the hell their team was, in front of what would almost certainly be a small crowd, not once but twice in two days.

The trip was memorable for a number of reasons. Colin had made the trip in place of Ricky. He substituted me with ten minutes remaining in the Friday night game. We were winning 2-0 and in complete control, so it was a chance for Phil to ease into the team. Unfortunately, he promptly surrendered two goals on two shots, the second in the final minute. After the equalizer, the Chattanooga team and their fans lost their collective minds in celebration, only

Chapter 12

to watch us kick off, string together a few passes, and score the winner with the last kick of the game.

The following afternoon, we killed time by driving to an attraction called Gem City. We parked the vans and walked a steep hill to the entrance, only to find the ticket prices too exorbitant. About face, back to the vans. Eventually it was time to head to the same stadium and play the same team again. Understandably, the crowd was about half the size this time, but the result was the same. This time I played just the first half, conceded a goal after thirty seconds, then watched from the bench as we won 3-1. After the flight to Orlando and the drive back to the Expo Center, Colin kept his promise and wrote me a check for $650. He handed it to me and we just looked at each other, each probably certain the other was in the wrong, before exchanging polite well wishes. I walked out the door and was no longer a Cocoa Expos player.

My relief was almost immediately tempered by guilt. Phil had looked like a decent, if inexperienced, keeper to me, so I didn't feel as if I had left the team in a bad situation. But it's never easy for a new player, especially a new goalkeeper, to get dropped into a team. Keith, Dylan, and Dave Mackey knew me, knew which balls I was going to come for and which I would leave, knew I could handle a ball played back to either foot. I, in turn, knew their tendencies and preferences. As a defensive unit, we clicked.

The Expos had won every game I played; they immediately lost the first two after I left. The losses were almost certainly unrelated to my absence, but it was an unfortunate fact, and my guilt grew. Keith told me that morale was low, that mutiny might be on the cards as anger over nonpayment finally bubbled to the surface. He gently told me that some players still committed to the cause resented my quitting. I pretended not to care, but I did. I

thought about Winston and Westy. What would they have
done? Surely they wouldn't have quit. But even if they
weren't being paid? I remembered what Lou Cioffi of the
Lions had said: It's a business.

Apart from when my conscience nagged me, I
enjoyed my post-Expos life. I spent more time at the beach
with my girlfriend, or alone in the wildlife refuge. I worked
earnestly on my novel. Minor, nagging injuries healed. The
Expos, after their two-game blip, got back to winning ways,
which mitigated my guilt. All was well – until Pat Dicks
called.

It was a Friday afternoon, hot and sunny as always. I
had already planned my weekend when the phone rang. Pat
was hesitant, then came out with it: they needed me for a
home game that night, the last game of the regular season.
He was vague about Phil, just said he "isn't available." My
instinct was to refuse, but I liked Pat, and also saw a chance
to redeem myself. It was only one game, I'd be doing them
a favor, and I wouldn't have to feel bad about quitting
anymore. So I agreed to play. Just one game, what could go
wrong?

It turned out to be the flashpoint game of the
season, with high comedy before, during, and after the
match. I pulled up to the Expo Center feeling very much
the hero, having responded to a call of distress to save the
day. The players greeted me warmly; if there was any
lingering resentment, they hid it well. I was feeling good
about my mini-return, ready to enjoy the one-night-stand as
a decent crowd started to roll in on a gorgeous late-summer
evening. Imagine my surprise, then, when Rick Sandt pulled
me aside and began to lecture me. He had hardly spoken a
direct word to me during the several months I was his
starting goalkeeper and we won every game I played, but he
seemed to have fundamentally misunderstood my presence

there. "I don't know how I can justify playing you tonight," he began. "You left the team and now you want to come back. I just don't know if it's fair."

I started to explain that I had been sitting in my office three hours ago, minding my own business, and was only in front of him now because Pat called and I agreed to help out in a pinch. But he wasn't looking at me as I spoke, and didn't seem to hear me; instead, he called Dylan over and said, "Dylan, how do you think the boys would feel about Justin playing?"

Dylan had been down this road many times with Sandt. He gave me a quick, reassuring look, and said, "I think they would be okay with it."

Sandt considered this, then looked back at me. "Here's what I think you need to do. We'll call the team together and if you apologize to everyone for quitting, you can play." He stood up and walked back into the dressing room to gather the players. I was so astonished I nearly laughed, but Dylan said, "Don't worry, he's done this a million times. Just say anything and it'll be over."

So with the team gathered in front of me, I blamed my stomach condition for quitting, and made a little joke that everyone laughed at, even though it wasn't funny. They found the whole thing as awkward as I did, and just wanted it to be over. I looked at Sandt, but he didn't say anything, so I stammered on for another minute or two, and finally just sat down. "Okay, go warm up," Sandt said, and we did. It was probably the worst pre-game speech I'd ever heard, and I had given it.

Despite how long it felt, I'd only been away from the team for three weeks, so I felt no real rustiness. I did, however, very nearly drop the clanger of a lifetime. An opposition defender (once again, I had no idea who we

were playing) cleared from inside his half, an enormous up-
and-under that plummeted down ten yards outside my box.
Nobody was chasing it and I had all day to collect, but when
it hit the turf, damped by evening summer dew, it skipped
forward unexpectedly. Next thing I knew, it bounded over
my head, as the crowd – naturally, we had a good crowd
that night – howled in terror. Time slowed and my senses
tingled. I could feel players from both teams thundering
behind me, but I was stunned into immobility. Finally, I
took off in pursuit and claimed the ball just before it
crossed the line, sliding along the cool turf and clutching it
to my chest. When I stood, the crowd was buzzing in
disbelief and Ricky laughed and shook his head at me from
the touchline. Disaster averted – just.

In the end, we won 2-1. The surreal scene in the
dressing room afterwards, with Dave Mackey leading the
player protest that was ultimately undermined by others still
loyal to Sandt, only confirmed my original decision to walk
away. I could now do it with no guilt. Ricky half-heartedly
tried to talk me into staying, but I couldn't get away from
there fast enough. This time I was really done. At home, I
told my girlfriend the story of the speech Sandt made me
give and the failed rebellion after the game, and we laughed,
relieved I was finished with them once and for all. For good
measure, I called Ricky to explain in detail why I couldn't go
on, just to make sure there were no hard feelings.

But the Expos were like a supernatural movie villain
who refuses to die. The following week, Pat Dicks called
again, this time with an appeal to join the team for the
playoffs – first a weekend in Birmingham, Alabama, and if
we won both games there, the following weekend in
Richmond, Virginia, for the league championship. Phil had
evidently left the team. Pat didn't elaborate, but I wasn't
surprised. They probably never paid him. I sighed. It would

be easy to refuse, but considering Keith and others were friends, difficult to justify. It was one thing quitting when they had Phil, but I couldn't leave them without any goalkeeper at all. Pat also promised to see to it that I would be promptly paid for every game. So I agreed, and like with every decision I ever made regarding the Expos, be it to play or not, I was immediately filled with deep misgivings.

My girlfriend was less ambiguous; she was angry. She had listened to me bitch and moan about the Expos for months, and supported the original decision to walk away. Now I was going to be leaving her home alone again for the next two weekends, in a town where the only other person she knew was my mother. It was the beginning of the end for us. The ice never thawed.

The original itinerary called for the team to drive up to Birmingham, a journey of six hundred miles, in a pair of vans on Friday evening for the Saturday night kickoff. Because of the late notice from Pat – his call came on Thursday – I told them I was too busy at work to leave Friday and insisted on flying up alone on Saturday. Colin surprisingly agreed with this, as it turned out he needed to fly up Saturday also, so he booked our tickets together. I was uneasy about this, but I found that away from the pressures of running the Expo Center under Sandt's ever-present gaze, he was relaxed and quite funny. Our flight was short and uneventful, and we had a nice conversation. We joined the rest of the team at the hotel before lunch.

Unbeknownst to me, I'd already made an incredible mistake. Because of the claustrophobia that had been rearing its head of late, I was in the habit of popping a Valium before flights. Our flights had always been the day before the game. It didn't occur to me that taking a Valium at eight in the morning would be problematic. But by the time we piled into rental vans for the drive to the stadium, I knew something was wrong. The pre-match nerves weren't there, and worse, I felt sleepy. I had already napped at the hotel for two hours after lunch, but it felt like my head was still back in bed.

By the time we kitted out and took the pitch for the warmup, I knew I was in trouble. My feet felt leaden, my legs dead, and I had no energy at all. Even after all that had happened, I did still take games very seriously, and always went through a methodical, exacting warmup, designed to physically prepare my body for the demands of the game, while simultaneously burnishing my confidence. My warmup in Birmingham did the opposite. I could barely move. I was going to be a liability.

The funny thing about this is that because I was drugged up on Valium, I wasn't worried. I figured it would all work out somehow, and coasted through the rest of the warmup with what must have been a dopey half-smile on my face. I caught one lucky break: there were four teams there, with the winner of both games advancing to the national semifinals the following weekend. For this first game, we'd avoided the home side and drawn a team from Des Moines. I had never been happier to play in front of an empty stadium.

We lined up at midfield for the national anthem. I kept shaking out my arms and legs, trying to get blood flowing and feeling restored, but I still felt like curling up and going to sleep right there on the pitch. I had a quick word with Keith and confided what was going on. He told Dylan and Dave Mackey that I wasn't feeling well and that they would have to play a bit deeper to protect me. Des Moines kicked off and I found it hard to follow play. Several times, I noticed I was standing right on my goal line with the ball seventy yards up the pitch. It was like falling asleep while driving: I shook myself out of it, jogged up to the top of the box, tried to move around, but minutes later it would happen again. The good news is that we were by far the better side, and carried a 2-0 lead into the final minutes of the first half. Even at that modest level of play, though, you just can't walk onto a pitch doped up and get away with it. Des Moines won a corner, the ball rattled around the box, and one of them hit it from fifteen yards. It was a decent shot, low to my left, but I saw it all the way and could already feel myself palming it around the post. Maybe I'd even hold it. Instead, I was still dropping to the ground as the ball zipped past me and into the net.

Happily, I felt the effects of the drug begin to wane at halftime. My head started to clear and my feet felt a bit lighter. It didn't make much difference, as we completely controlled the game and I had nothing to do in the second half. Afterward, Keith gave me a sage piece of advice: "Don't do that again."

The next night we played Birmingham, the home team. The crowd arrived early. They sat close to the pitch, boisterous and loud. A couple of drunk rednecks behind my goal heckled me mercilessly. I knew they were hoping for some kind of response, so I ignored them. We began uncertainly, and I had a few saves to make, but we gradually took control of the midfield, and, therefore, the game. Shortly after halftime, Kirk Mackey headed us into the lead. A second followed a few minutes later, silencing the crowd, but just as it looked like we were home and dry, Birmingham sprung our offside trap and left me no chance with the finish. The drunk redneck crowd came back into it, baying at every challenge, and I picked the worst time of the season for my only real mistake.

As often happens when a team is under pressure, we began giving away silly fouls, including one in a dangerous position near the corner of the penalty area to my left.

Instead of shooting or whipping in a cross, the Birmingham player floated a simple ball directly to me. I shouted for it, confidently climbed above a challenge to claim it – and watched in horror as it slipped right through my gloves. I twisted back and grasped for it as I fell, but could do nothing to stop a Birmingham player from lashing it on the volley at the empty net. Only it wasn't empty; Dave Mackey hurled himself across the line and blocked it with his chest. Minutes later, we put the game out of reach with a third goal. On the stroke of full time I saved one of those bizarre USISL "seventh foul" penalties, which made me feel a little better about the dropped cross, but the important thing is that we'd won.

Of course, the downside of winning is that the season continued on, a final pair of games the following weekend in Richmond. I had no sense of perspective. It was only another week, but to me it seemed an eternity, a life sentence. It kept me awake all night in the hotel. Once the adrenalin of the match wore off, and after I replayed the dropped cross a hundred times in my mind, I couldn't help but think that losing would have been no tragedy. I knew it was wrong to feel this way, and my guilt compounded the rollicking emotions. At three in the morning, I slipped out of my hotel room and walked the drab property for two hours. I had wild fantasies of walking away into the night, letting the team pile into the vans and drive back without me. I was in conflict, generally not wanting to play anymore but still taking pride in my performances and finding the odd moment of enjoyment during games, but it was a bigger issue than that; it was a matter of identity. Up until my last game at Borehamwood, I identified myself primarily as a goalkeeper. But now I was a writer, one with counter-cultural aspirations and affectations (I hadn't cut my hair in nearly a year). The concepts of competition, discipline, and

Chapter 12

commitment, minimum requirements even at this modest level of the game, not only no longer came naturally to me, but seemed downright anathema to the person I felt myself becoming. I was betraying my teammates by my lack of enthusiasm, but felt I was betraying myself just by being there. I felt trapped. That feeling, along with the loss of power that came with it, was a strong trigger for panic attacks. Knowing that, and anticipating them, made it even worse.

Fatigue finally sent me trudging back to my room. I slept for a few hours before joining the team at breakfast, feeling sheepish. In my strange state of mind, my dropped cross was emblematic of my unsettled state. I imagined everyone looking at me, wondering what was wrong. The prospect of a ten-hour drive home in a van was depressing, but I heard Kirk Mackey talking about getting a cheap one-way flight home. After a few phone calls, we learned we could fly home for $115 out of pocket. The flight was just under an hour. Even with my claustrophobia, I wasn't about to choose a ten-hour van ride over a one-hour flight. A few of us joined Kirk and bought the tickets. Our flight wasn't until later in the afternoon, so we went to the Birmingham Zoo until then.

I stared at the alligators for an hour. Again, I had an urge to simply stay. On top of everything going on with the Expos, my relationship at home was crumbling under my feet. My girlfriend and I didn't fight, but we barely spoke, either, living as roommates instead of intimates. We were marking time, wondering who would be the first to pull the trigger. As loathe as I was to spend ten hours in a van, I wasn't much more excited about going home.

13

The final week of training crept along. I made the best of it, working hard, determined to play well. Since I had committed to the bitter end, we might as well win the championship. Despite everything, the attitude in the team was positive. Nobody had said much about it, but the plan seemed to be to play and win and then simply hope Sandt made good on our contracts. The positivity lasted until the day before we were to depart for Richmond.

The original itinerary called for us to fly, but this changed to an overnight trip on a "luxury bus". A few players grumbled, though it didn't sound bad to me. When we gathered at the Expo on Thursday morning, however, we were met not with a luxury bus, but the same two familiar white vans we had crossed the southeast in so many times. By this stage it wasn't surprising, but it started the trip off on a sour note that would only worsen.

Colin drove one van, Pat Dicks the other. I was in Pat's van. The plan was to spend the night at a hotel a little more than halfway to Richmond, then finish the drive in the morning. We drove in tandem for a while, but eventually a gap opened. We reached the hotel after seven hours, fifteen minutes ahead of Colin. Richmond was only another three hours down the road, so we talked Pat into pressing on. We wanted to sleep in and have the entire morning to rest and relax. Pat agreed, but he couldn't get Colin on his phone. After agonizing over it for a few minutes, he decided to keep driving. We cheered, but Pat was tight-lipped. He knew he was going to catch hell from Colin, and a few hours later, when we arrived in Richmond, he did. I overheard him on his phone, trying to defend his decision, but Colin was apparently furious. I felt for Pat, but it was a price that had to be paid. It would have been silly to finish the drive the morning of a game.

We played the first semifinal on Saturday at five o'clock, against some team from Mississippi. I rarely knew who we were playing. From the start, the USISL overwhelmed me. There were far too many teams to keep track of, most of them from second-tier cities. The host side, Richmond Kickers, played San Francisco in the evening's second game. Arby's sponsored the Kickers, and for the weekend they extended their sponsorship to the entire Final Four, which meant our team got to eat at Arby's for free. But not at any Arby's; only one specific branch. At three o'clock, we were still driving around Richmond trying to find it.

Fast food obviously does not make for a great pregame meal, though we all understood the finances and nobody complained. But it was far too close to kickoff to be eating anything heavy, let alone pseudo-roast beef sandwiches that had been sitting under heat lamps all day. Fortunately, the team from Mississippi turned out to be about as good as you might expect a team from Mississippi to be, and we won without much trouble.

Toward the end of our match, the stadium began to fill up in advance of the Kickers' game, and by the time they kicked off, they had eight thousand fans there. We watched the game from the press box. At halftime, feeling restless, I walked downstairs and watched the rest of the game alone, from a less-crowded part of the stand. Right there, in the middle of the second half, with the noise of the crowd swelling and cresting with each chance, I had something close to a panic attack. I needed to get away from everybody. Not just my teammates, but from everyone else, too. I tried to focus on the game, but ended up pacing back and forth along the concourse at the top of the stadium. I forced myself to breathe deeply and slowly, and eventually my racing heart and mind both settled.

I wanted Richmond to win, despite the obvious advantage they'd have against us by playing at home, because I wanted my last game to be in front of a decent crowd. There was no question in my mind that tomorrow would be the last game I ever played. The game went to extra time and San Francisco wasted numerous chances, before the Kickers won it with a goal at the death. So it was set: Cocoa Expos vs. Richmond Kickers for the championship of the USISL, my last game ever.

The panic attack took something out of me, and I fell asleep early back at the hotel. In the morning, finally tired of carrying a ridiculous mane of hair on my head all summer, I found a barber shop near the hotel and got a few inches hacked off. At noon, we gathered in the lobby and made the trek back to Arby's, where I immediately lost my appetite. Business as usual: over the course of the season, I'd had a decent pregame meal no more than five or six times. I sipped a bottle of orange juice to keep my blood sugar up, and relied on adrenalin for the rest. As much as I wanted the game and season – and my career – to be over, I was nervous. I wanted to win.

I've always been an empiricist. I don't believe in fate or destiny, I don't believe "everything happens for a reason" and I don't have superstitions. But I do believe that athletic performance can be hampered by negativity, and there was no question that we as a team, and me in particular, came into the final under a vortex of negative energy. The season-long dispute over player payment was still ongoing; we were all annoyed by the long trip in vans and the pregame meals at Arby's; and now, right before

Chapter 13

kickoff, as the teams lined up at midfield after the national anthem had been played, the referee told me my jersey was too similar to Richmond's kit, and I had to change.

I ran back into the dressing room, in the bowels of the small stadium under eight thousand fans, and dug through my gear for an alternate jersey. I found one, rushed back out, and within twenty minutes, we were down 2-0.

In all the games I'd played, we'd never lost, and only been a goal down a few times. But the Kickers had us in deep shit. They were a classic "sum greater than the whole of the parts" team, a group of slightly-above-average players who ran, covered, and competed ferociously for each other. They went close twice in the opening exchanges, then forged ahead when I fell prey to over-thinking. A diagonal ball over the top picked out a Richmond player clean in on goal, but I could see he was going to have a hard time controlling it. It was coming from over his shoulder and he was on a dead run, so before it even got to him, I belted off my line, ready to clear when his touch was inevitably less than perfect. It was the kind of anticipation and reading of the game that only comes from years of competitive play, born of thousands of hours of training, watching, and learning. It was the kind of decision-making that separated me from the mostly amateur-level goalkeepers in this league. And it turned into a nightmare.

I was correct that the Richmond player would not be able to take down the through ball cleanly. But what I failed to anticipate is that he would completely fucking miss it. I sprinted straight out at him, about ten yards and closing as he jumped to take his touch with the inside of his right foot, but somehow the big lumbering goon just missed it, completely wrong-footing me. The ball ran off toward the corner flag, and, committed, I had no choice but to chase after it with him. He got there first, just outside the box with his back to me, and I had a snap decision to make: try to tackle him like an outfield player, or sprint back to goal. I chose the latter, figuring he still had work to do to make something of the chance. He spun and crossed over me, right onto the head of a Richmond player rushing into the box. He thumped a header behind me as I scrambled back into goal. The crowd roared as I lay sprawled on the turf. One-nil, Richmond.

It got worse. Richmond had a goal mysteriously disallowed, another powerful header from a right-wing cross, then minutes later repeated the trick from the opposite wing. This time we got no help from the ref. After twenty minutes we were 2-0 down, the crowd braying and jeering us as we stood around looking at each other in disbelief. I was forced into a good save when their left winger twisted his way into the box and unloaded a shot across me towards the top corner, and we charged down and scrambled away a couple of other dangerous chances. After those near misses, we went close at the other end, somehow failing to score when their keeper dropped a looping cross right onto the line. Still, halftime came as a reprieve for us, as the Kickers continued to keep us on the back foot.

We improved in the second half, and got a goal back after a neat exchange of passes. Despite feeling as if we'd taken a hammering, we were only a goal down, and suddenly chances to equalize started falling our way. But we couldn't find the finish we so desperately needed, and predictably, Richmond caught us on the break and scored a third to put the game away. I made one more decent save late on, which at least gave me something to feel good about, before it ended 3-1.

I had time for reflection toward the end, knowing it was my last game at any sort of organized level, time to look around at the crowd, the cones of summer mist under the massive floodlights, the green, dew-slicked grass. I saw all these things, but didn't feel anything. I just wanted it to be over, which only highlighted how far out of love I'd fallen with the game. But it wasn't that, really. I still loved the physical sensations of playing: turning a rasping drive over the bar, diving around like a little kid during finishing drills, the warm satisfaction of a sweetly struck goal kick or a cleanly handled cross. It was everything else: being part of a team when it apparently didn't suit my personality, the small-time, rinky-dink leagues, and most critically, the loss of control regarding travel, daily schedule, and eating. My stomach problems only exacerbated this, making me resent being forced to eat at certain times or away from home so often. Over just a handful of years, I'd morphed from an eager-to-please neophyte with the Lions, dazzled by the romanticism of the game, amazed to be a teammate of the great Winston DuBose, to a distant and reserved loner. The problem was clearly me, not football. But it was easier to just quit playing than to fix myself.

We went out drinking in Richmond after the game, then drove home in the vans in the morning. Several players nursed hangovers. I was relaxed; it was finally over. I found myself enjoying the company of my teammates, or former teammates. Still, when we arrived back at the Expo Center after dark, I didn't linger long, just said a quick round of goodbyes and headed home.

It was not a clean break. It never is. The Expos, to their credit, threw a team dinner at the Cocoa Beach Pier. Colin suggested we take it in turn to each say a few words, and without exception, each one of us used the opportunity to praise Ricky and thank him for all he did for us. He'd been put in a nearly impossible situation, being manager in practice but not in name, having to defer to Sandt on occasion, and with the morale of his squad torpedoed by the payment fiascoes. He handled it all with grace and class. My chief regret, though I didn't say this, was that I hadn't had a chance to play for him a few years earlier, before whatever had happened to my love for the game happened.

There was also the matter of the final check owed to me, for the last two weekends of playoff games. I knew by now that it was a waste of time going to anyone but Ian Gill, our midfielder who worked at the Expo Center as the comptroller. He knew when the bank balance was positive. I called him once a week to check, and finally, after nearly two months, he told me to come in. I cashed the check, paid a few bills, and drove over to Cocoa Village, a scenic street of vintage and specialty shops in historic buildings along the Indian River. I bought a calzone from an Italian pizza joint and ate it in a waterfront park, watching for dolphins, the sun dappled and warm on my face.

14

I had always wanted to live in the Florida Keys, a tropical island chain dripping off the southern tip of the state into iridescent waters just ninety miles north of Cuba. The Keys stood for everything I wanted: health, warm winters, beauty, exotic tropicality, and literary bohemianism. It didn't matter that I'd never actually been there. I'd seen pictures, and that was enough; I wanted to live there.

A few weekends after the season ended, my girlfriend attended a wedding in North Carolina. Without planning, I jumped in my car that Friday and drove three hours south to my brother's place in Miami, spent the night, and drove into the Keys early Saturday morning. I was underwhelmed at first; for thirty minutes, there was nothing but strip malls and tourist bars. But once I left Key Largo behind and saw the water for the first time in Islamorada, a mix of lime green and electric blue, I was hooked. I camped for the weekend at Bahia Honda State Park in the middle keys, sleeping in the back of my SUV under a canopy of coconut palms. I snorkeled all day in the crystalline ocean, marveling at clouds of brightly colored tropical fish that let me swim right through them. The stars at night, unhindered by city lights, glimmered as thickly and brightly as they had when I was on foot safari in South Africa. By Sunday evening, as I reluctantly drove back to my brother's place, my mind was made up. Whatever job I might have to do, whatever hovel I might have to live in, I was moving there, alone. I had just turned twenty-nine years old. I'd finish my novel, it would be published, and I would live the writer's life in the Florida Keys.

Chapter 14

And that's exactly what happened.

Epilogue
The Brooklyn Gunners

A biting wind blows down the pitch straight into my face. Though it is only the first week of December, New York is soaked in a midwinter freeze. Temperature at kickoff is twenty-seven degrees Fahrenheit. Inside my gloves, my fingers tingle and then go numb. Players on both teams bounce and jump, blow into their hands, waiting for the referee to blow his whistle. My stomach pulses with nerves and excitement. It feels good. I've missed it.

Twelve years had passed. I bounced from the Keys to a job as a fulltime goalkeeper coach in North Carolina and back to the Keys again. I finally completed my undergraduate degree. My third stint in the Keys, living on a boat, was ended by a series of scary, near-miss hurricanes in 2005. Feeling the need to leave my comfort zone, I applied to, and was accepted by, the graduate creative writing program at New York University. The phobia that had manifested in me avoiding my teammates and seeking solitude had long since evaporated. I loved living in the middle of teeming Manhattan. It was while there, in 2007 at the age of 40, my love of goalkeeping unexpectedly came flooding back.

I'd had many opportunities to step back in goal while coaching, and I sometimes took them. But over the course of a dozen years, I never played an actual game, nor had any interest in doing so. The principle reason was that I was simply tired of it, but I also wasn't about to dive around on the kind of weedy, rock-strewn dirt bowls that amateur teams play on. But I was intrigued by the new 3G artificial turf that I saw around New York City. It was soft and yielding, thanks to the base of shredded rubber. As I explored the city, I saw that almost all the public parks and recreation spaces had this turf in place. I found myself lingering to watch the games being played there, and with plenty of time on my hands – I was in the writing program on a part-time basis – I decided to give it a try again. I placed an ad on Craigslist, announcing that I was a goalkeeper in search of a game. Everybody needs goalkeepers.

I joined a seven-a-side team and was predictably rusty at first, but eventually started making half-competent saves. After a dozen games, I was ready for something more substantial. Another Craigslist ad landed me with the Brooklyn Gunners, a collection of young professionals competing in the Gotham Soccer League, full 11 v 11, ninety-minute games. My first appearance was a disaster: we lost 7-0 to a much better team. I was at fault for two of the goals. Worse, my right leg locked up later that night, a victim of the strain of twenty or so goal kicks. I was plagued with doubts, but decided to give it a few more games. We lost the next game just as badly, but I played a little better and ached a little less. Gradually, everything improved. I even kept a clean sheet one night. My teammates became my friends – close friends. We weren't great, but everyone worked hard and we had a terrific time playing. We played Spring, Summer, and Fall seasons, skipping only the coldest months of January and February. We played late at night, not finishing until midnight, sometimes at Pier 40, a convenient walk from my East Village apartment, but more often at Randall's Island, where I had a view of the Chrysler Building from my goal.

I fell totally, and without reservation, back in love with goalkeeping. It wasn't like when I was with

Borehamwood or the Lions, trying to make a living, but all the way back to when I was a kid, building the Dust Bowl in my back garden. Any spare money went toward gloves and equipment. Gloves had advanced during my twelve-year hiatus; new styles and latexes and brands had emerged, and I couldn't wait to try them all. I felt young and fast and light some nights, old and slow others, but it was always fun. I joined an online goalkeeping forum and discussed gloves and training and games with other keepers from all over the world, including one who recognized a picture I posted and sent me a message: "Justin – you played for the Orlando Lions against Dunfermline Athletic? I was the other goalkeeper that night!" Mick McAdams, the Dunfermline keeper I shared the shootout with, is a friend now.

I finished grad school, moved in with a woman, got a dog. I stayed in New York and kept playing for the Gunners, the oldest player in the league by some margin. 42, 43, 44, 45, 46. My relationship ended, she let me keep the dog, I moved to a new apartment in Brooklyn.

I have regrets. I wish I had gone for it more when on trial at Brentford and Dunfermline Athletic. I wish I had risen above the pettiness in that final season with the Expos. I wish I had talked to a professional about my fears and phobias when I had been in their grip. There are mistakes and misjudgments, and simple bad luck, from twenty-five years ago that I still catch myself thinking about.

I *still* can't believe that Richmond player completely missed his touch.

But then I think: I was just a skinny kid from Florida who ended up with his boyhood hero for a teammate, who had nights in European stadiums with cheering crowds, who saw the game from the inside in a way not too many people get to. I didn't do too badly.

Epilogue

John Hillcoat once told me about an old pro who said to him, "Football is 95% blood, sweat, and tears. But the other 5% makes up for it."

I'm not even sure I ever had the other 5%. But I still agree.

Soccer Tough by Dan Abrahams

"Take a minute to slip into the mind of one of the world's greatest soccer players and imagine a stadium around you. Picture a performance under the lights and mentally play the perfect game."

Technique, speed and tactical execution are crucial components of winning soccer, but it is mental toughness that marks out the very best players – the ability to play when pressure is highest, the opposition is strongest, and fear is greatest.

Soccer Tough demystifies this crucial side of the game and offers practical techniques that will enable soccer players of all abilities to actively develop focus, energy, and confidence. Soccer Tough will help banish the fear, mistakes, and mental limits that holds players back.

Scientific Approaches to Goalkeeping in Football: A practical perspective on the most unique position in sport by Andy Elleray

Do you coach goalkeepers and want to help them realise their fullest potential? Are you a goalkeeper looking to reach the top of your game? Then search no further and dive into this dedicated goalkeeping resource. Written by goalkeeping guru Andy Elleray this book offers a fresh and innovative approach to goalkeeping in football. With a particular emphasis on the development of young goalkeepers, it sheds light on training, player development, match performances, and player analysis. Utilising his own experiences Andy shows the reader various approaches, systems and exercises that will enable goalkeepers to train effectively and appropriately to bring out the very best in them.

Graduation: Life Lessons of a Professional Footballer by Richard Lee

The 2010/11 season will go down as a memorable one for Goalkeeper Richard Lee. Cup wins, penalty saves, hypnotherapy and injury would follow, but these things only tell a small part of the tale. Filled with anecdotes, insights, humour and honesty - Graduation uncovers Richard's campaign to take back the number one spot, save a lot of penalties, and overcome new challenges. What we see is a transformation - beautifully encapsulated in this extraordinary season.

Saturday Afternoon Fever: A Year On The Road For Soccer Saturday by Johnny Phillips

You might already know Johnny Phillips. He is a football reporter for Sky Sports' Soccer Saturday programme and a man who gets beamed into the homes of fans across the country every weekend.

For the 2012/13 season, Johnny decided to do something different. He wanted to look beneath the veneer of household-name superstars and back-page glamour to chronicle a different side to our national sport. As Johnny travelled the country, he found a game that he loved even more, where unheralded stars were driven by a desire to succeed, often telling stories of bravery and overcoming adversity. People who were plucked from obscurity, placed in the spotlight and, sometimes, dropped back into obscurity again. Football stories that rarely see the limelight but which have a value all fans can readily identify with.

CPSIA information can be obtained at www.ICGtesting.com
Printed in the USA
BVOW081938030713

324985BV00001B/23/P